THE ART OF
GLASS

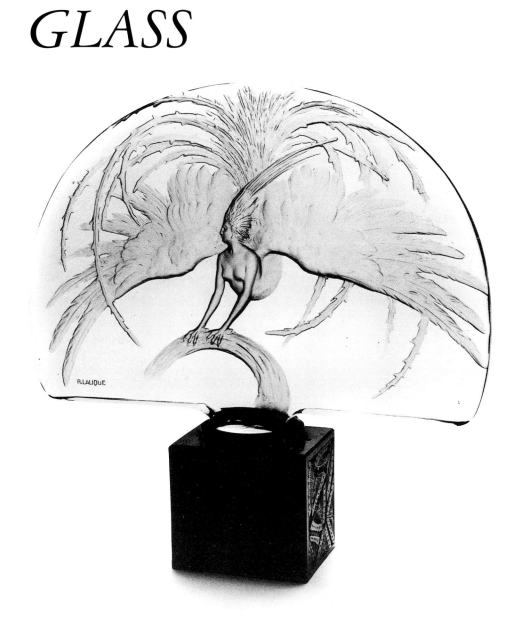

ART NOUVEAU TO ART DECO

THE ART OF
GLASS

Victor Arwas

with contributions by Susan Newell

ANDREAS PAPADAKIS PUBLISHER

Publisher's Note: I should like to express my thanks to all those at Tyne & Wear Museums, especially to Susan Newell for her painstaking work in researching and collecting the material for the *Art of Glass* exhibition at the Sunderland Museum and Art Gallery and for preparing the appendices of this book, and to Councillors Don Price and Ralph Baxter, Chairman and Vice Chairman of Tyne & Wear Museums Joint Committee, and Dr David Fleming, Director of Tyne & Wear Museums for their help in making this publication possible. My special thanks to Victor Arwas for writing the main essay and being unstinting with his help and advice at all times. Without the support of Tyne & Wear Museums Corporate Patrons Scheme, the City of Sunderland and Northern Arts there would not have been a book to accompany this imaginative exhibition and so our thanks to them and to all those individuals and institutions who have lent such wonderful exhibits, especially to Galerie Moderne for the Lalique material. AP.

FRONT COVER: RENE LALIQUE Vase bacchantes in opalescent glass, model created in 1927. H. 25, Marks R. Lalique France. Collection Mr. and Mrs. Vincent, courtesy of Galerie Moderne, London; BACK COVER: LOUIS C. TIFFANY & CO. Favrile lava vase, c. 1900. H.15.5, Marks 9926C L. C. Tiffany Favrile. Haworth Art Gallery, Accrington (Hyndburn Borough Council); PAGE 1: RENE LALIQUE Surtout de table, oiseau de feu, table lamp in clear glass, intaglio moulded with a firebird design, on a patinated, cast bronze base with a design of butterflies. H. (including base) 43, Marks R. LALIQUE, Manchester City Art Galleries; PAGE 2 : LOUIS C. TIFFANY & CO. Favrile iridescent gold vase with green leaf and vine motif, c.1900. H.23, Marks 3318 P Louis C. Tiffany - Inc. Favrile, Haworth Art Gallery, Accrington (Hyndburn Borough Council); PAGE 3: RENE LALIQUE Car mascot Victoire, also known as 'Spirit of the Wind'. model created in 1928. W. 25.6, Marks R. Lalique, Private Collection, courtesy of Galerie Moderne, London; PAGE 6 : RENE LALIQUE Vase quatre grenouilles formant pieds, cire perdue,1922. H. 18, Marks R. LALIQUE, Private Collection, courtesy of Galerie Moderne, London: PAGE 7: JULES HABERT-DYS Massive bulbous glass vase fused with metallic shreds all over its surface, c. 1913. H.22, Mark J. H. D. Formerly in the collection of the Marquis de Pourtalès, Robert Zehil, Private Collection, Monaco

All measurements throughout this book are given in centimetres

First published in Great Britain in 1996 by
ANDREAS PAPADAKIS PUBLISHER
An imprint of Cranbourne Investments Limited
Kilbees Farm, Hatchet Lane, Windsor, Berks SL4 2EH

ISBN 1 901092 00 3

Printed and bound in Singapore

CONTENTS

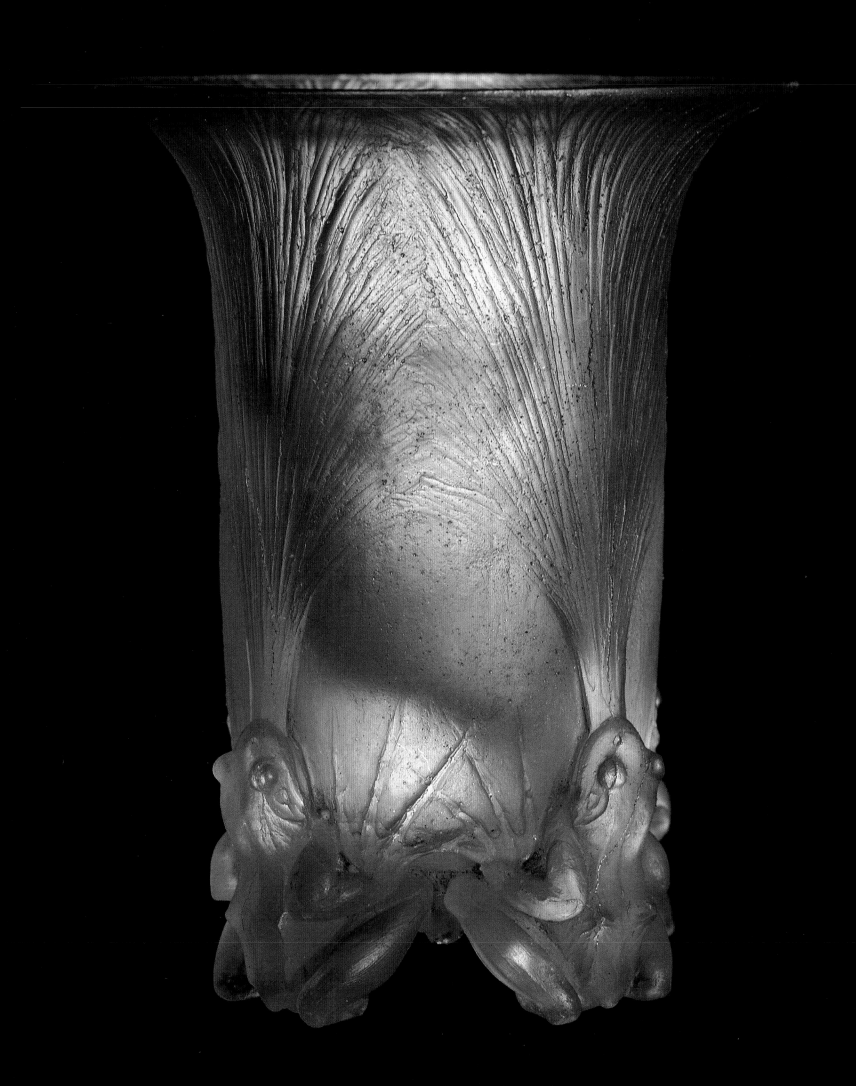

GLASS BLOWER

Foreword and Acknowledgements

Tyne and Wear Museums is delighted to have been able to collaborate with Andreas Papadakis on the production of this book, which is published to accompany the *Art of Glass* exhibition at Sunderland Museum and Art Gallery. The exhibition includes many pieces of Art Nouveau and Art Deco glass, many never previously seen on public display, and is Sunderland Museum's major contribution to the Year of Visual Arts 1996. Sunderland has a long and continuing tradition of glassmaking, and the exhibition puts the Museum's displays of Sunderland-made glass in the context of European glassmaking for the first time.

We are extremely grateful to Victor Arwas, the leading expert on Art Nouveau and Art Deco glass, for his involvement in the project by writing the text for this book and by lending important works for the exhibition. The Director of Galerie Moderne, Mark Waller, also deserves special thanks for advising on and arranging the Lalique loans and for allowing extensive use of Galerie Moderne's photo library. We would especially like to thank all the anonymous private lenders and all those who have helped including: Brian Cargin, Martine de Cervens, Mrs. Chesldene, Kevin and Ina Harris, Chris Morley, Mr. and Mrs. Moty Levy, Mr. and Mrs. Napier Robson, Adrian Norris, Mr. and Mrs. Vincent, Mrs. Sharman, Ian Turner, Sheila de Vallée, Barbara Woroncow and Robert Zehil.

Museum colleagues nationwide have provided invaluable assistance including: Stella Beddoe, Rosalyn Clancey, Roger Dodsworth, Glenys Evans, Virginia Glenn, Chris Meechan, Jennifer Opie, Jennifer Rennie, Catherine Ross, Ruth Shrigley, Gary Topp, Tracey Taylor and Karin Walton. Also Sir Geoffrey de Bellaigue, Sir

Alastair Aird and Caroline Paybody facilitated the organisation of the royal loans. Others who deserve thanks include Lisa Lams and David Hillery.

Tyne & Wear Museums photographer, Les Golding, has photographed the loans from the public and private collections of British and Scandinavian glass and also the Arwas and Zehil loans. Barry Stacey of Lightworks photographed the Tiffany glass at the Haworth Art Gallery and Matt Pia photographed the Habert-Dys vase.

Susan Newell, Assistant Keeper of Fine & Applied Art for Tyne & Wear Museums, has played the major role in researching and organising the exhibition with assistance from Nick Dolan, Keeper of Applied Art. She has also written the Dictionary, Glossary and Appendix.

This book and exhibition have been made possible by generous financial support from the Tyne & Wear Museums Corporate Patrons Scheme 1996, the City of Sunderland, and Northern Arts. Additional funding was provided by the prestigious National Art Collections Fund award for the 'Best New Project' for Sunderland's Glorious Glass display in 1995 at the Museum and Art Gallery.

Councillor Don Price
Chairman of Tyne & Wear Museums Joint Committee

Councillor Ralph Baxter
Vice Chairman of Tyne & Wear Museums Joint Committee

Dr. David Fleming
Director of Tyne & Wear Museums

**T&WM
TYNE & WEAR
MUSEUMS**

7: FRANÇOIS-EUGENE ROUSSEAU *Cameo vase of transparent glass with internal sprays of red, white, yellow and blue oxides and silver foil, wheel-carved with a North African townscape, overlaid with an opaque red layer, itself wheel-carved with an Arab boat and an oasis with palm trees and a camel and rider, c. 1880. H. 12.4. Victor Arwas Collection, London;* **8**: *ERNEST-BAPTISTE LEVEILLE Transparent glass vase with red and green inclusions, crackled and martelé, cased in beige glass carved and incised with flowers and leaves, c. 1895. H. 36, Marks E. Léveillé Paris. Formerly in the Barrelet Collection. Robert Zehil, Private Collection, Monaco;* **9**: *PHILIPPE-JOSEPH BROCARD Vase in clear glass with applied purple lip and enamelled tortoise design, c. 1885. H. 16. Broadfield House Glass Museum, Hulbert of Dudley Collection*

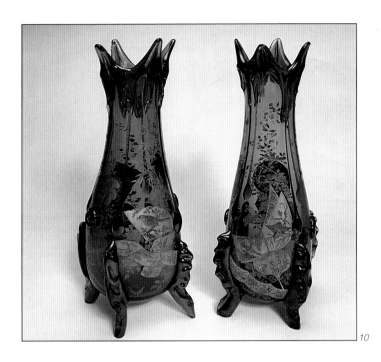

10: *AUGUSTE JEAN Pair of baluster vases in glass, each resting on four applied feet, the necks pulled up to points, alternating with others running down, two large glass cabochons applied to the sides with a Japanese polychrome enamelled design, gilt, c. 1878. H. 57, Mark A. Jean. Robert Zehil, Private Collection, Monaco;* **11**: *THOMAS WEBB AND SONS Bowl engraved by William Fritsche and enamelled by Jules Barbe in the Japanese style, 1880s. H. 10.8cm, signed W. Fritsche and Marked Webb, Broadfield House Glass Museum, Kingswinford;* **12:** *JAMES POWELL & SONS LTD. Vases in straw opal, c. 1900. H. left 27, right 20, Brian Cargin and Chris Morley Collection*

PRECURSORS

Looked at objectively, the creation of Art Glass in the nineteenth century was an anomaly. After all, the prime purpose of research into glass production was to achieve clarity and purity. As Auguste Daum put it, "One has absolutely no idea of the extent of the scientist's knowledge, the glassblower's art and the manufacturer's competence required to create a fine pub glass. It has to be very clear to give the liquid its exciting colour, voluminous in aspect to attract the customer, thin at the rim to feel pleasing to the lips, thick-walled for when it is empty, and, finally, very heavy for use in legitimate self-defence."

Curiously the most interesting experiments in the production of what was basically non-functional Art Glass took place in Paris rather than in the traditional centres of glass production in France. And most were not carried out in glasshouses but by individuals working in small studios. One of the most interesting was PHILIPPE-JOSEPH BROCARD who trained as a restorer of antiques and objets d'art. He became fascinated by Islamic mosque lamps, which he collected and studied, and he spent several years experimenting with enamelling on glass and with glassmaking procedures and techniques. Once he had totally mastered the existing ones he went on to discover and patent several more. He executed a dazzling array of mosque lamps, vases, bottles, ewers and plates of Turkish, Persian, Arab and Moorish inspiration using interlaced patterns and Arabic script - generally Koranic quotations.

In addition to these Orientalist patterns, he produced vessels inspired by the Renaissance as well as Greek and Roman decoration. He first exhibited, with great success, at the 1867 International Exhibition in Paris. Other exhibitions followed in Vienna and Paris, and he was awarded a First Prize in Paris in 1878. Emile Gallé

was a fellow exhibitor and was greatly impressed by the enamels of Brocard, which he promptly adopted, adapted and transformed. Brocard, too, was greatly impressed by the work of the young Gallé, and soon began producing enamelled versions of plants and flowers. In 1884 Brocard's son Emile became his partner, and they retailed their enamelled glassware, which now included such *tours de force* as enamelled glass tables, through the showroom of Edmond Enot in the Avenue de l'Opéra.

Another important enameller on glass was AUGUSTE JEAN. In the 1870s this ceramist and potter, son of a distinguished ceramist, began creating glass vases enamelled with Persian subjects, which soon gave way to Japanese ones. Using exceptionally clear glass in various colours, polished to a striking standard, he increasingly decorated his vessels with rims, bases, feet or handles, intricately twisted, kneaded or sculpted with a variety of tools either at the kiln or using lampwork techniques. The surface was then enamelled and frequently gilt. He enlarged his repertory with opaque vessels, translucent ones with coloured metallic oxides trapped within the glass layers, and yet others with externally applied glass cabochons and insects, which were then enamelled in his intricate, often asymmetrical manner, and sometimes at an angle, askew. His final style eschewed enamelling, producing vessels of extraordinary purity in which the freely-wrought glass decoration is itself the form, thus anticipating much contemporary glass by nearly a century. Nothing is known about where he learned his techniques or where he executed his vessels, although it is likely that he hired a bench, possibly with some workers, at the *Cristallerie de Clichy* in Paris. He was very successful at the 1878 Paris Exhibition, where the *Conservatoire*

14

des Arts et Métiers (the Arts & Crafts Museum) purchased a fine group of his works. In 1885 he ceased working with glass as mysteriously as he had begun, and returned to ceramics.

In 1855, FRANÇOIS-EUGENE ROUSSEAU (1827-1890) took over the family retail ceramics and glass shop at 41 rue Coquillère in Paris, succeeding both his father and his grandfather. In 1867 he commissioned a dinner service from the painter and etcher FELIX BRACQUEMOND. It consisted of over 200 different designs of fish, crustaceans and animals in a Japanese style derived from Hokusai. It was immediately popular and sold in his shop for several years. Encouraged by this success, he determined to experiment with glass. He hired two of the greatest glass designers, makers and engravers of their era, EUGENE MICHEL in 1867 and ALPHONSE-GEORGES REYEN ten years later.

Michel engraved table glass and crystal vases and bowls with Japanese ornaments and floral patterns, while Rousseau himself spent more and more time at the glassworks of Appert Frères. Founded at Clichy in 1835 by Louis Appert, it was then run by his two sons, Adrien and Léon, who turned it into one of the most successful glassworks of the period in France. Léon was of the most eminent glass technicians of his day, and wrote several technical books on the subject with Jules Henrivaux. Appert Frères produced a wide variety of glass for every purpose, from stained glass windows to wall cladding, optical glass, laboratory glass, reinforced glass and some art glass. Although Rousseau was technically illiterate, his artistic concepts and enthusiasm prodded the Appert brothers to experiment ceaselessly to produce new and vibrant colours. Victor Champier wrote in 1891 in the *Revue des Arts Décoratifs*, "They invented for him a whole palette

running from blood red to pale violet, and made for him vases that looked like precious stones: the richness and hardness of agate, opaline softness, mother of pearl reflections, onyx iridescence." The blood red, in particular, was resistant to fire.

All Rousseau's early vessels were executed by Appert Frères and, even when he opened his own glass-making studio, he continued to consult them on technical matters, as indeed did many other glass designers and makers, including Gallé and Daum. Rousseau designed and made a wide variety of vessels, some in carefully composed shapes, others in extraordinary free forms that alternated thin with thick-walled glass, transparent pastel colours with opaque ones, applying sections to the outside from detailed insects to elephant-head handles, perfecting the technique of internal crackling by plunging the hot parison from the kiln into a bucket of cold water. As his mastery of the medium increased, he combined several techniques in a single vessel. The full range of his creations was shown at the 1884 Paris Exhibition organised by the *Union Centrale des Arts Décoratifs*, which later established the present Museum of Decorative Arts. He exhibited *hors concours* (a great honour, placing him above those whose entries were eligible for prizes) and was awarded the *Légion d'Honneur* later that year.

The following year Rousseau sold his shop to his former pupil and assistant, ERNEST-BAPTISTE LEVEILLE (1841-1913). Most of Rousseau's vases were unsigned, but some that were in stock were signed at Léveillé's instigation. Rousseau stayed on until 1888, when his health forced him to retire, and he died two years later. Léveillé changed the name of the business to Rousseau & Léveillé Réunis and moved the premises to 74 Boulevard Haussmann. He also added his name

15: left APPERT FRERES Vase designed by Ernest-Baptiste Léveillé, clear glass with coloured and gold inclusions, wheel-cut and internal crackled decoration, 1889. H.16.5; right ERNEST-BAPTISTE LEVEILLE Mould-blown vase with coloured inclusions and internal crackled decoration, c.1893-94. H. 17.7. Courtesy of the Trustees of the V. & A.; *16*: STEVENS AND WILLIAMS Moss Agate vase, c. 1888. H. 13.5. Broadfield House Glass Museum, Kingswinford; *17*: STEVENS & WILLIAMS Silveria vases, c. 1900. H. left 22.3, right 13.3, Broadfield House Glass Museum, Kingswinford

19

18

to all the signed pieces, and invariably signed his own. He continued to use Rousseau's techniques in his own vessels, although his shapes were often more tormented, and occasionally of Art Nouveau inspiration. Shortly after 1900 Léveillé merged with *Maison Toy*, which had a prestigious address at 10 rue de la Paix. He produced some fine tableware marked *Toy & Léveillé*, but the beginning of the twentieth century was financially difficult, and he was forced to sell the business to Haraut and Guignard, the owners of *Le Rosey*. Haraud-Guignard continued to produce existing Léveillé designs for some years, signing them with either the initials *HG* or *Le Rosey*. Léveillé himself died totally forgotten in 1913. The works of Léveillé and Rousseau, considered separately or together, remain one of the creative summits of glass production in the late nineteenth century in France.

Unlike France, the production of art glass in England was led not by individual artists, but by established glassworks and firms of decorators. The Excise Act of 1745, which had imposed an onerous tax on materials used in the manufacture of glass, was repealed in 1845, and the 1851 Great Exhibition at the Crystal Palace, followed by many other major international exhibitions throughout Europe and the United States, encouraged old glasshouses to expand and new ones to set up. Factories were increasingly concentrated around Stourbridge, Birmingham and Dudley, and perceived Victorian prosperity encouraged many glassworkers and designers to migrate to them from France, Italy, Portugal and Bohemia. Later in the century many more glassworkers emigrated from Europe to the United States, joined by several British workers.

Various coloured glass techniques were developed in these glassworks, of which the most extraordinarily detailed was the revival of *cameo glass*, each example a *tour de force* of the carver's art and technique, often using tools he had made himself. The brothers John and Joseph Northwood and John's son John II, George Woodall and his brother Thomas, Joseph Locke and William Fritsche were among those who produced breathtakingly realistic images in carved glass. But these inevitably took a very long time to execute, and were consequently very expensive. They therefore tended to be commissioned as special exhibition pieces. Nevertheless, their attraction for the wealthy was such that in order to satisfy the demand the glassworkers were forced to devise simplified production methods, including the use of hydrofluoric acid to etch the basic pattern, simpler decoration - often floral - using fewer layers of glass, and the use of a carving wheel rather than hand tools.

Various attempts at producing silver-looking glass were made. Freederick Hale Thompson and Edward Varnish of E. Varnish & Co. patented a process in 1849 in which double-walled glassware was silvered on the inside and layered on the outside with coloured glass which could then be intaglio-cut to reveal contrasting coloured and silver patterns. Similar attempts were made by other firms, some using silver or gold foil, but in 1900 JOHN NORTHWOOD II devised a layered glass vessel with enclosed silver foil, the inner vessel blown almost to its full size before being coated with the foil, cased with an outside layer of clear glass, then finished with trailings of coloured glass over the surface. The outside layer was sometimes allowed to split and air bubbles to explode, thus allowing bits of the enclosed foil to oxidise and discolour, adding to the overall effect. This technique, called *Silveria*, was made by the firm of Stevens & Williams. William Stevens and Samuel Cox

21: *JAMES COUPER AND SONS* Clutha glass, c.1880-1900. left Vase in green with cream streaks and gold aventurine inclusions, design attributed to Christopher Dresser. H. 19.4. Crafts Centre, Middlesbrough Borough Council; centre Vase in clear glass with silver mica inclusions, possibly designed by George Walton for James Couper and Sons. H. 20. Brian Cargin and Chris Morley Collection; right Liberty & Co. pewter vase with Clutha liner in green with gold aventurine inclusions, designed by Archibald Knox as part of their Tudric range. H. 15.3. Crafts Centre, Middlesbrough Borough Council

Williams had taken over the Moor Lane Glass House at Briar Lea Hill (which later became Brierley) near Stourbridge in 1847 and built it up into a major glassworks rivalled only by Thomas Webb & Sons at Stourbridge.

A wide range of decorative glass was produced at Stevens & Williams, including *Tapestry Ware*, *Jewell Ware*, *Threaded Ware*, *Intaglio Ware*, *Matsu No Ke*, and *Moss Agate*. The latter was developed by JOHN NORTHWOOD in the late 1880s, and consisted of blowing a gather of light soda glass, coating it with a layer of heavier lead glass, rolling the parison onto a layer of multicoloured powdered glass, then pulling the powdered glass thus picked up into random patterns using a hook; it was then reheated, coated with a further layer of lead glass, and given its final shape; the vase, still hot, had water rapidly poured over it and was drained, crackling the soft soda glass; again reheated, the crackled glass took on the internal *Moss Agate* patterns. FREDERICK CARDER, who later became co-founder and artistic director of the Steuben Glassworks in Corning, New York, designed many of the *Moss Agate* vase shapes, which were often cut and polished.

Thomas Webb & Sons also produced a vast range of decorative glass, including *Bronze*, *Peach Bloom*, *Queen's Burmese*, *Old Roman*, *Satin* and *Tricolour*, though much of their production consisted of cut lead crystal, which their successor Webb Corbett still produces, maintaining its fine quality. The firm employed at various times the Woodall brothers, John Thomas Fereday (who worked there for some forty years), Daniel Pearce and his son Lionel, Frederick Englebert Kny, a Bohemian engraver, and his three sons, Ludwig, Harry and William, William Fritsche (c.1853-1924), also a fine Bohemian engraver who spent some fifty years at

Webbs, and Jules Barbe, a Frenchman who ran a gilding and enamelling shop.

The Glasgow glasshouse of *James Couper & Sons* developed a new type of decorative glass in the 1880s. Internally bubbled and streaked, the shaped vessels had no external decoration other than the occasional handle or spout. Made by rolling a gather of lightly coloured glass over some powdered coloured glass and flecks of mica with occasional shreds of silver foil or aventurine, it was then reheated and shaped according to the designer's instructions. Patches of opaque coloured glass were sometimes combed into feathered patterns in the glass. This glass was given the name *Clutha*, based either on an ancient Scottish word that meant 'cloudy' or on the ancient name of Glasgow's River Clyde.

In the late 1880s CHRISTOPHER DRESSER (1834-1904) was employed as principal designer at Couper's. Born in Glasgow, he had published several books on botany, ornamentation and design, as well as designing quantities of metalwork, ceramics, fabrics, carpets, wallpaper, silver and plate, and cast iron. He had taken examples of British design to the new Japanese National Museum, and purchased many Japanese artefacts for Tiffany & Co. in New York as well as for himself. His designs for *Clutha* are often based on Roman, Middle Eastern and Peruvian patterns, although he also produced free shapes that can vary from the awkward to the utterly successful, from the earthbound to the sublime. Dresser designed *Clutha* glass until the mid 1890s, after which Couper hired GEORGE WALTON (1867-1933), an architect and designer, who tended to use richer colours than Dresser, making liberal use of aventurine and gold flecks, although with less adventurous, rather more symmetrical shapes.

ART NOUVEAU

Art Nouveau is a somewhat confusing term to the neophyte. For a start, it is not a new art. It is the name of S. Bing's Paris Gallery, which had for several years brought the art of Japan and China to France. Bing had become friendly with a group of young artists, disciples of Gauguin, who were collectively known as the *Nabis*. He had been to the United States on behalf of the French government to report on the state of the arts there. He had met and become friendly with Louis Comfort Tiffany, introduced him to the *Nabis* and to Toulouse-Lautrec, and Tiffany had commissioned them to execute designs for stained glass windows. Bing transformed his gallery, which became a showcase for the fine and decorative arts, and called it *L'Art Nouveau*, meaning contemporary art. It was an amalgam of influences: Japanese imagery and sensibility, Symbolist Idealism and Idism, the worship of Beauty, admiration for the Arts & Crafts concept of the superiority of the hand over the machine and, above all, the return to Nature, the naturalistic interpretation of flora and fauna, not the stylised nineteenth-century approach based on a misunderstanding of Classicism.

EMILE GALLE was undoubtedly the greatest designer of glass at the turn of the century. Indeed one defines Art Nouveau glass as by Gallé or inspired by Gallé or derived from Gallé, though there were, of course, many other very talented glass designers. His apprenticeship was long and covered many different aspects of creation and design. Born in Nancy, in the East of France, in 1846, he was a prize pupil at the local Lycée Impérial and took courses in botany, drawing and landscape painting. His father, Charles Gallé, had married Fanny Reinemer, whose father had recently died, leaving a retail shop that sold ceramics and glassware. Charles soon took over the running of the shop, the name of

which was changed to *Veuve* Reinemer et Gallé then, in 1856, to Gallé-Reinemer. After some years of retailing other people's products, Charles opened a decorating studio in Paris, then moved closer, opening a studio in the old *Faiencerie de Saint-Clément*, whose 18th-century reputation had badly declined. He revived it by introducing charming decoration on the blanks supplied by the factory, and then commissioning an array of new shapes, including cats, rabbits, owls, pug dogs and heraldic lions, mostly designed by Gengoult Prouvé whose son, Victor, though younger than Emile Gallé, became a very close friend and associate. Charles also commissioned table glass from the Saint-Denis and Pantin Glassworks, but in 1864 he opened a glass decorating shop in Meisenthal, in the Sarre Valley, and began collaborating with a fine local glassworks, Burgun, Schwerer & Cie, also known as the Verrerie d'Art de Lorraine, then run by Mathias Burgun.

In 1862, Emile was sent to Germany by his father to study mineralogy, art history and botany in Weimar, where he was introduced to the music of Franz Liszt and Wagner. He returned to Nancy in 1864, spent a year working with his father, then went to Meisenthal, where he spent the next three years studying all the glass techniques in use there, spending considerable time in the firm's laboratories learning about the chemistry of glass. Within a year of his arrival he was given his own workshop in which to carry out his own experiments, and became close to Mathias Burgun's son, Antoine, and the firm's brilliant young designer, DESIRE CHRISTIAN. In 1870 the Franco-Prussian war broke out. Emile volunteered, but the war soon ended with the defeat of France and the loss of Alsace and a sizeable part of Lorraine, which were annexed by Germany. Meisenthal and Saint-Clément were now in German

Verrerie Parlante Vase: A snow covered scene with birds in a landscape, wheel-carved, etched, enamelled and gilt with the verse:
L'Hiver laboure les sillons de nos coeurs
La neige maternelle a couvert leurs semailles

Gallé

[Winter ploughs the furrows of our hearts
The maternal snow has covered their seed]

Gallé

23

22: *EMILE GALLE Symbolist vase with applied cabochons over silver foil, wheel-carved with a large flying bat, the reverse carved with the sun about to rise over a sleepy village. This superb vase, designed and executed shortly before Gallé's death in 1904, illustrates that slightly sinister twilight world when bats fly, seen only by ghouls and ghosts. Gallé was then seriously ill, and was preoccupied with death. H. 37.5, Mark Gallé. Courtesy of the Trustees of the V. & A.; **23**: EMILE GALLE Verrerie Parlante Vase, c. 1900. H. 45. Victor Arwas Collection, London; **24**: GALLE GLASSWORKS (Cristallerie d'Emile Gallé) Vase in amber glass with cased and acid-etched decoration of leaves with wheel-carved details and applied green berries, c.1920. H. 30.5, Mark Gallé. Broadfield House Glass Museum, Kingswinford*

24

25

territory. Emile visited London where he studied the glass in the British Museum and the South Kensington Museum, now the Victoria & Albert, and spent some time in the Royal Botanic Gardens in Kew. This was followed by a study of the collections in the Paris Museums, before he went to Raon-l'Etape to work for Adelphe Muller, a family friend, who owned a ceramics factory.

In 1873 Charles Gallé purchased a large property in Nancy, La Garenne, in which he built both the family home and the family works. Emile promptly returned and set up a glass decoration studio. Within a year Charles had closed down the ceramics decoration studio at Saint-Clément and transferred it and the men who worked there to La Garenne, moving the ceramics manufactory to Raon-l'Etape in 1875. That same year Emile married a pastor's daughter and took increasing control of the family firm.

In 1885 Emile Gallé signed a contract with Burgun, Schwerer & Cie and Désiré Christian undertaking to give them regular work: the glassworks was to execute vessels and Christian was to decorate them and sign them *Gallé* in accordance with Gallé's specific and detailed drawings, moulds and instructions. They were to share technical secrets and discoveries; blank glass was to be supplied to Gallé at a discount; all the designs were to be his exclusive property; and they all undertook to keep secret their agreement, which was to last for ten years.

Gallé believed that the use of hydrofluoric acid was vulgar, and that vases should be transparent, colourless or palely tinted, and decorated with traditional patterns in black and gilt or occasional enamelling. He spent considerable time developing different tints for glass, of which the most successful and imitated was *Clair de Lune*, a pale blue made with potassium and cobalt

oxide that turned a brilliant sapphire when struck by light. He first exhibited at the 1878 Paris Exhibition, where he took over a whole pavilion, and was awarded four Gold Medals. He was fascinated by the *cameo* glass exhibited on the English stands by John Northwood, Alphonse Lechevrel and Joseph Locke; the intricate enamels of Joseph Brocard; the iridescent effects achieved by the Pantin Glassworks; and the seemingly endless effects achieved by Rousseau. It was clear to him that no single treatment of glass made sense, and he was the spend the rest of his life exploring the possibilities.

He essayed every type of enamelling, opaque and translucent, enamel jewels and enamel over metallic foil, priding himself that "there is now no shade, however evanescent, which my palette of relief enamels on glass cannot reflect, from orange and sealing-wax red to violet and purple." He designed Brocard-style enamelled vases but gave them additional depth by etching the glass to make the enamel stand out. "Do glassmakers not have the ability to knead their own agates, marbles and rock crystals?" he wrote, and produced a range of glass 'hardstones' in the appropriate colours, some of which were intaglio-carved, enabling him to refer to himself on occasion as a 'counterfeit lapidary'.

Tokouso Takashima, a Japanese botanic artist, spent the years between 1885 and 1888 in Nancy. He and Emile became firm friends, and the Japanese artist instructed Gallé in brush techniques and the simplifications and stylisation of Japanese art. La Garenne was set in grounds in which a huge variety of plants and flowers grew, surrounded by wild flowers and giant cow parsley, the *ombelles* that inspired so many of Gallé's designs. He spent many hours making superb drawings of the flora, and also studied, drew and used a

26

vast number of insects, particularly the dragonfly, moth, butterfly, and other somewhat more sinister things that happened to flutter by.

Gallé's designs were complete in every detail. The shape of the vessel and the complete decoration were drawn in detail, with several manuscript pages describing the type of glass required, its colour or colours, the precise number of acid baths needed, where the wheel-carving should be applied. He even specified the precise signature that was to be used. In his increasing desire to personally supervise every detail, he decided to transfer the production of glass to La Garenne. Antoine Burgun supervised the construction of a kiln round which ten glass blowers could work, and this was lit on 31st May, 1894. Gallé employed the finest workers available, and they immediately went into full production. In order to finance the high cost of research and production of his artistic output, Gallé launched a parallel line of 'industrial' glass. Much of the early production was carried out at Meisenthal, but was then continued in Nancy. It was mostly acid-etched, sometimes also wheel-carved, consisted of several layers of coloured glass, of which the outermost was the darkest, and was decorated in cameo with various landscapes or, more often, different flowers or plants, always botanically accurate and drawn naturalistically. He became increasingly involved with botanical research, corresponded extensively with scientists in France, Belgium, Switzerland, Germany, England and the United States, became the leading light of the Nancy Central Horticultural Society, whose *Bulletins* he regularly wrote, and he wrote and published almost a hundred articles and speeches. At the International Botanic Congress held in conjunction with the Universal Exhibition in Paris in 1900 he presented a paper on the orchids of Lorraine.

27

27: *EMILE GALLE Free-blown iridescent glass vase, the marquetry trees framing village houses, the whole set into a free-form applied base, c. 1899. H. 25. Private collection;* **28**: *EMILE GALLE Rose de France free-blown footed vase, internally decorated, externally applied with roses, buds and stems in high relief, c. 1903. H. 24. Private collection*

28

29: DAUM NANCY Vase in pink with enamelled and gilt design of thistles, c. 1895. H. 8.4, Marks Daum Nancy with the Cross of Lorraine. The Royal Pavilion, Art Gallery and Museums, Brighton; **30**: DAUM NANCY Jug in green with acid-etched and gilt decoration, c. 1895. H. 24.5, Marks Daum Nancy and the Cross of Lorraine. Courtesy of the Trustees of the National Museums of Scotland

31

When the ten-year contract with Meisenthal expired it was not renewed, although he remained friends with Burgun and Christian, and was a shareholder in Burgun's glassworks when it went public. His business continued to expand: he opened a carpentry workshop producing serial furniture as well as extremely expensive pieces; and a metal workshop, where he produced bronze and wrought iron lamp fitments and bases.

Gallé's industrial production was issued in thousands of examples; most of the artistic pieces only in about five or six examples, often with individual variations. Some special commemorative designs were made in single examples. He was extremely well read and was involved with the Symbolist movement. In his inaugural speech on his election to the Stanislas Academy in Nancy in 1900, he said: "Those masters of the verb, the poets, are also the masters of decoration; they have the genius of the image, they create the symbol." Many of his images were inspired by poetry, and he sometimes quoted a line or two of poetry on his vases, which he called *Verrerie Parlante* (Talking Glass). He also attempted to recreate in glass some of the effects of light imagery achieved by the Impressionists on canvas. Using a variety of techniques, including marquetry, in which slivers of glass of one colour were inserted into the body of the vessel while still hot (a very fraught technique which he patented, and which depended on matching the coefficient of expansion of the different glasses as they cooled), and various effects created in the kiln with metallic or other oxides and vapours, he created extraordinary vessels which he called *vitrified poems*. These were greatly admired in the various International Exhibitions, and Proust himself wrote two poetic descriptions of Gallé glass in *The Remembrance of Things Past*.

The 1900 Exhibition was a great, though expensive triumph for Gallé, who exhibited in five separate sections. His glass exhibits included the recreation of a kiln surrounded by some finished vases and many damaged and broken ones, showing the precarious nature of glassmaking. He was awarded two *Grands Prix* (the highest awards) for his glass and furniture and was made a Commander of the *Légion d'Honneur*. In addition, Gold, Silver and Bronze Medals were awarded to several of his workers.

A year later, on 12th February, 1900, the School of Nancy was formally inaugurated. This Provincial Grouping of the Art Industries had been his idea and he became its President with Antonin Daum, Louis Majorelle and Eugène Vallin as Vice-Presidents. In March 1903 the School of Nancy exhibited in Paris at the Pavillon de Marsan, but the exhibits of the six founder members were swamped by seventeen other exhibitors including manufacturers of lace and fabrics, leather, beaten metal panels and stained glass.

Gallé had been showing signs of exhaustion since the 1900 Exhibition, and he was in and out of clinics, sanatoriums and spas. As soon as he returned to Nancy he would plunge back into work, preparing for the forthcoming 1905 Paris Exhibition. On 23rd December, 1904, he died of leukaemia. His father Charles, who had carried on working to help his son, had died almost exactly two years earlier. Gallé's friend Victor Prouvé succeeded him as President of the School of Nancy, which survived until 1914. Gallé's widow Henriette took over the running of the factory, and ordered that all new glass be signed *Gallé* with a star as a mark of respect and mourning. The Gallé works turned out Emile Gallé's designs, executed by his workers, until 1914. Indeed, Madame Gallé managed to increase the number of glassworkers to some 500, double the number in 1901. In 1914 Henriette Gallé died. War broke out. Gallé's three daughters felt unable to take over, so one of his sons-in-law, Paul Perdrizet, a history schoolteacher, succeeded her. For many years the firm continued to produce the old designs of industrial glass, mostly for export. In the late 1920s the sons-in-law finally hired some designers, and began production of some new designs, in particular several blow-moulded floral and fruit vases, some with polar bears, penguins, otters, elephants, eagles and other animals and a number of vases enamelled all over with a single bright colour such as red or yellow and with a single enamelled motif of a dragon or animal. The international crisis that followed the New York stock market crash of 1929 led to the closure of the Gallé works in 1931, although the liquidators took several years to disperse the contents. Parts of La Garenne were sold off over the years, and all the documentation held in the works was destroyed.

The example of Gallé was instructive to several other glass factories. JEAN DAUM (1825-1885), a solicitor and Deputy Mayor of Bitche, was forced to flee with his family as the German forces advanced in 1870 and eventually annexed Alsace and part of Lorraine. He settled in Nancy and lent some money to a new glass-works which went bankrupt, and he found himself its proud owner. With no technical knowledge or business experience, he only managed to get out of trouble by marrying the daughter of the founder of the Nancy gasworks, who brought a sizeable dowry. Their sons Auguste (1853-1909) and Antonin (1864-1930) in turn came to the rescue. Antonin joined the firm in 1887 straight from the prestigious Ecole Centrale where he took an engineering degree. He took over production, while Auguste ran the business side. They concen-

32

34

35

33: *DAUM NANCY Vase designed by Henri Bergé with mould-blown design of autumnal chestnut leaves, coloured with vitrified powders and wheel-carved, c. 1908. H. 41.3, Marks Daum, Nancy with Cross of Lorraine. United Group International SA, courtesy of Galerie Moderne, London;* **34**: *MULLER FRERES Table lamp in cameo glass, acid-etched in cameo with an all-over pattern of red poppies on a blue ground, c. 1905. H. 67.3. Marks on base and shade Muller Frères Lunéville. Victor Arwas Collection, London;* **35**: *DAUM NANCY Cameo table lamp in cased red and brown glass, acid-etched with a dense riverside landscape with large trees in the foreground, c. 1910. H. 46.3, Marks Daum Nancy with Cross of Lorraine on the shade and with the monogram on the base. Victor Arwas Collection, London*

trated on watch glass and table glass, but were influenced by the array of Art Glass exhibited at the 1889 Paris Exhibition. A year later Antonin, who was bedridden at the time, began to sketch various vases with floral decoration, and he soon had them executed. Pleased with the result, the Daums increasingly produced Art Glass, adopting ever more adventurous techniques and developing several of their own.

Vases were acid-etched and wheel-carved, often making use of facetting the surface with tiny shallow cuts to produce a *martelé* effect similar to that of a lightly hammered metal plate. In 1899 they patented a system of decorating the surface of the inner layer of a vase, then overlaying it with one, two or more layers of different coloured glass. This gave the inside decoration an additional dimension of depth. Autumn scenes could thus have rain trapped within the walls of the vase. A landscape could, with reheating and manipulating, become a landscape in a storm, the trees bending in the wind. Many of the vessels were decorated with plants and flowers, some of the most effective being blown into moulds to give a three-dimensional effect to trees or leaves, then finely etched or wheel-carved. Abstract surfaces were created by a process called 'vitrification', in which the parison was rolled over powdered coloured glass on a marver, then reheated until this ground glass vitrified on the surface, which was left rough. This surface could then be etched, polished, left rough or otherwise treated to achieve various effects. Still another of their techniques, called *Verre de Jade* (Jade Glass) or *Céramique de Jade* (Jade Ceramic) was similar to vitrification, but then had a layer of clear glass blown over it. This gave a curiously modern, abstract look to the vessel, and was copied by many other glassmakers all through the 1920s.

The MULLER FAMILY stands out as one of the more interesting glassmakers in the Art Nouveau style. Nine brothers and one sister were born in Kalhausen in the Moselle department in Lorraine, an area entirely devoted to glassmaking. The older children were apprenticed at the nearby Saint-Louis glassworks, but when the German army occupied the area in 1870, the family fled to Lunéville, where they entered various glassworks and perfected their skills. From 1895 the two eldest, Désiré and Eugène, went to work for Emile Gallé, closely followed by Henri, Victor and Pierre. In 1895 Henri left Gallé to set up on his own at Lunéville. His blanks were blown to his precise requirements in a small glassworks, the Gobeleterie Hinzelin at Croismare, near Nancy, and decorated in his little studio. Soon the entire family joined him, displaying their phenomenal skills in carving and engraving, devising extraordinary vases with as many as seven different glass layers deeply carved to create three-dimensional landscapes. They also created a new technique of bonding enamel to a glass vessel then acid-etching it to achieve painterly effects of colour, which they called *fluogravure*. In 1906 Georges Deprez, director of the Val-Saint-Lambert glassworks in Belgium invited Désiré and Henri Muller to introduce a new range of glass 'in the style of Emile Gallé.' In fact, they did not copy Gallé, but created a new range of Muller-inspired vases. Working closely with LEON LEDRU, a fine designer at the Val, they provided 411 different models in less than two years. All were in fluogravure, which they taught to the Val's workers, and were in a wide variety of shapes and colours. All were decorated with the naturalistic floral designs that Gallé and, indeed, the School of Nancy, had made their own.

In 1908 the Mullers moved to larger premises in Lunéville as business expanded. They generally signed

36: *left, Auguste Daum, right, Antonin Daum;* **37**: *Daum Glassworks 1894, Packing Shop;* **38**: *Daum Glassworks in 1894;* **39**: *DAUM NANCY Pedestal dish in glass applied with a silver-gilt rim cut with honesty hovering over the bowl, c.1900. H. 9.6, Mark freeform signature* Daum Nancy *with Cross of Lorraine. Victor Arwas Collection, London*

all wheel-carved pieces *Muller Croismare* or just *Croismare*. Etched pieces were normally signed *Muller Frères Lunéville* or *Muller Lunéville* or just *Lunéville*. Because of the denseness of the fluogravure material, the signature was sometimes concealed within the colours on the base. Muller designs for the Val were invariably signed with the initials *VSL*, frequently in twisted lettering.

When war broke out in 1914, Lunéville was occupied by the Germans, and the Mullers again had to flee. Eugène was killed at the front. The others dispersed, and went to work for various glassworks. After the Armistice in 1918 the survivors drifted back to Lunéville, purchased the Hinzelin works and went back to work.

Although they continued the tradition of executing vases in Art Nouveau styles, these were but pale copies of their prewar creations. Their more 'modern' production, which included many light bowls and table lamps in frosted glass and Art Deco designs, became very successful, and by the late 1920s they were employing some 300 workers. The Depression forced them to stop production in 1933, and they closed down permanently in 1936.

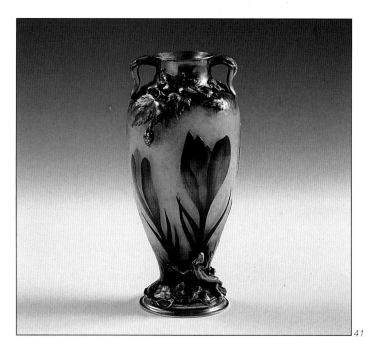

40: DAUM NANCY Cameo glass vase, wheel-carved and etched with catleya orchids and leaf design, with a matching wrought silver rim, partly martelé ground, c. 1900. H.19, Mark Daum Nancy with Cross of Lorraine. Victor Arwas Collection, London; **41**: DAUM NANCY Cameo vase etched with crocuses applied with silver-gilt mounts at rim and at the foot, with a silver-gilt lizard, c.1900. H. 21.8, Mark Daum Nancy with Cross of Lorraine, mounts with French silver hallmarks. Victor Arwas Collection, London; **42**: MULLER FRERES Multilayered glass pitcher, decorated in fluogravure with a shepherdess and her flock, etched and wheel-carved over enamel, with applied handle, c.1900. H. 20. Mark Muller Croismare. Formerly in the collection of Dr. Henry C. Blount, Chattanooga, Tennessee, USA. Robert Zehil, Private Collection, Monaco

43: LOETZ (Glasfabrik Johann Loetz-Witwe) Candia Papillon *vase with silver mounts, designed by Henri Van de Velde and executed for Meier Graeffe's* La Maison Moderne *in Paris, 1900. H. 13.9. Victor Arwas Collection, London;* **44**: MULLER FRERES *left Multilayered glass vase decorated in fluogravure with flowers and leaves, etched and wheel-carved over enamel, c. 1900. H. 7, Marks Muller Croismare; right Multilayered glass pitcher, decorated in fluogravure with an owl and several bats, etched and wheel-carved over enamel, applied handle, c.1902. H. 16.5, Marks Muller Croismare. Victor Arwas Collection, London;* **45**: VAL ST. LAMBERT *Vases designed by Henri and Désiré Muller. left Multilayered glass decorated in fluogravure with chrysanthemums, c.1903. H. 26.3, Mark VSL; centre Vase decorated in fluogravure with hydrangea, c. 1906. H. 27.7, Mark VSL. right Vase decorated in fluogravure with blackberries, c.1906. H. 17.4, Mark VSL. Victor Arwas Collection, London*

IRIDESCENCE

Iridescent glass was used by various glasshouses in the late nineteenth century: Pantin in France, Webb in England and Lobmeyr in Austria among them. But it was not until Tiffany in the United States and Loetz in Bohemia became involved in its production that its great and varied possibilities were truly explored.

LOUIS COMFORT TIFFANY's father, Charles Lewis Tiffany, had founded and built up a New York store into an important retail operation, importing and selling jewellery, silver, sculpture and giftware, but also manufacturing elaborate silver vessels, flatware and jewellery. He also formed an exceptional collection of gemstones.

Louis graduated from the Flushing Academy on Long Island, spent two years studying painting with George Innes, then went to Paris to study with Léon Bailly, an Orientalist painter. He visited London, where Tiffany & Co. had just opened a branch in Regent Street, then travelled to Spain, North Africa, Egypt and Italy with Samuel Colman, a fellow American artist. He returned to New York in 1870 and showed the paintings he had done abroad in his studio. A year later he was elected an associate of the National Academy of design, was a founder-member of the Society of American Artists in 1877, and was elected a Full Member of the National Academy in 1880. He exhibited his paintings in Tiffany & Co.'s stand in Paris in 1878 when the company was awarded a Gold and six other medals; and in Philadelphia at the Centennial Exhibition, where it received a Gold Medal and seven other awards. He was invited to lecture at the New York Society of Decorative Arts.

With the family fortune behind him he could have spent the rest of his life as a dilettante painter. He chose instead to join with Lockwood de Forest, Samuel Colman and Candace Wheeler to found Louis C. Tiffany & Associated Artists, hired an army of trained craftsmen and women, and set out to decorate the homes and yachts of the very rich, as well as several theatres and a group of rooms in the White House in Washington. Coordinated wallpaper, fabrics, wall hangings, bed covers and embroidered linens, and tapestries and furniture were executed in his workshops, while he scoured the world for antiques and objets d'art.

He purchased coloured panes from various New York glasshouses for assembly into leaded glass windows in his workshops, but was disappointed in the quality and range of colours available and so hired chemists to research different effects, using the Brooklyn glassworks of Louis Heidt for the purpose. He eventually developed a range of rich colours and one of special effects, including different textured glass, sandwiched panes, either against each other or with a space between them, and panes with folds and other finishes.

In 1882 Associated Artists separated from Tiffany & Co. Two years later Tiffany became a widower, and as the decorating business had slowed down, he devoted much of his time to New York's night life. In a bid to wean him away from this life his father commissioned him to decorate a large town house on Madison Avenue and 72nd Street. Louis promptly set to work, founded the Tiffany Glass Company, and married again the following year. In 1889 Tiffany accompanied his father's chief designer Edward C. Moore to Paris for the International Exhibition, where he saw the glass of Gallé and Loetz for the first time. Moore, a fervent collector of Oriental works of art, introduced him to Samuel Bing, the greatest Parisian dealer in such works. In 1892 Tiffany formed the Tiffany Glass & Decorating Company for the "manufacture and sale of glass, decorative objects and materials of all descriptions, and the applying of these materials to buildings and other structures; also the manufacture and sale of furniture, house and church fittings of all kinds, and the conducting of a general decorating business."

Bing went to New York to make a survey of American art and industry on behalf of the French Government, and spent considerable time with Tiffany, who had been considering exhibiting some paintings at the forthcoming Columbian World's Fair in Chicago. Bing persuaded him that he should produce something sensational, and Tiffany designed and manufactured a complete chapel, which became the Fair's biggest attraction and brought him a total of fifty-four medals.

Tiffany's meeting with Arthur J. Nash (1849-1934), former manager of the White House glassworks, a Webb subsidiary in Stourbridge, led to his incorporating the Stourbridge Glass Company in 1893. With fresh funds from his father he built a new glassworks at Corona, Long Island but as soon as it was built it was destroyed by arson. Tiffany rebuilt it. The glassworks was run by Nash, later helped by his two sons. Two glass shops were set up, one for the production of cathedral glass for assembly in leaded glass windows, the other a glass blowing shop headed by Tom Manderson. As business expanded more glass shops were opened, each complete with a gaffer, a blower and server, a decorator, a mixer, a gatherer, and two or three boys to assist. Several workers came from the Boston and Sandwich Glass Company, which had gone bankrupt after a strike, while others came from England. There was also a research laboratory with several chemists headed by Tiffany's friend Dr. Parker McIlhiney. Tiffany was president and artistic director. He would bring in sketches on scraps of paper to the design office which had the task of drawing them up in detail. He also brought in ancient vessels from his private collection to be copied.

46

48

47: *LOUIS C. TIFFANY & CO. Favrile reactive* glass vase, c. 1900. H.12.5, Marks *1139 L. C. Tiffany Favrile Exhibition Piece.* Haworth Art Gallery, Accrington (Hyndburn Borough Council); **48**: *LOUIS C. TIFFANY & CO.*, Favrile paperweight vases, left *H. 10.3, Marks 99225C L.C. Tiffany Favrile,* with original paper label *Glass Registered Trade Mark LCT* monogram; right *H. 20.7, Marks L.C. Tiffany 6662 B Favrile,* with original paper label in black and white *Glass Registered Trade Mark LCT* monogram. Haworth Art Gallery, Accrington (Hyndburn Borough Council)

Tiffany was fascinated by iridescence, the property acquired by ancient glass which has been buried in the sand for centuries, a curious glow which occurs as the glass reaches the end of its life. In a booklet published by the firm in 1896, Sir David Brewster's words are quoted: "There is perhaps no material body (glass) that ceases to exist with so much grace and beauty, when it surrenders itself to time and not to disease." Tiffany had obtained a patent for *lustred glass* as early as 1881, and he set his chemists to work to achieve a highly-polished set of iridescent, mostly opaque colours. The first vases produced at Corona were of laminated glass in imitation of agate, similar to those exhibited by Loetz at the 1889 Exhibition in Paris. They were soon followed by decorated vases with some lustre.

Bing had transformed his shop in Paris to *L'Art Nouveau*, and he commissioned Tiffany to execute a number of leaded glass windows to drawings by Pierre Bonnard, Eugène Grasset, Henri-Georges Ibels, Paul-Elie Ranson, Ker-Xavier Roussel, Paul Sérusier, Henri de Toulouse-Lautrec, Félix Vallotton and Edouard Vuillard. He later commissioned more Tiffany windows from drawings by Frank Brangwyn which were exhibited with other works from *L'Art Nouveau* at the Grafton Galleries in London. Bing became Tiffany's exclusive concessionaire in Paris while Tiffany & Co. had the concessions in London and New York. Tiffany maintained the exclusivity of his glass by supplying only a limited number of fashionable luxury retail stores throughout the United States. They received his wares on consignment for three months. Unsold items were then returned to Tiffany who sent them on to a different consignee. Glass returned unsold after being sent to three consignees was normally smashed.

Tiffany exhibited glass in Munich, Brussels and Budapest, and many museums purchased it, the Victoria & Albert in London as early as 1896. As business expanded, so did the range of his products. He opened a foundry and metal shop for the production in bronze and copper of desk sets, inkstands, candelabra and candlesticks, boxes, and lamp bases and fittings. His earliest lamps had blown glass shades, but he soon expanded into leaded glass shades, which became phenomenally successful.

He also began the production of mosaics, used on small metal articles, on some elaborate lamp bases, and on such massive undertakings as large murals, including one from a design by Maxfield Parrish for the Curtis Publishing Company in Philadelphia. A glass mosaic curtain for the National Theatre in Mexico City comprising two hundred three-foot-square panels with a hydraulic raising and lowering mechanism took twenty men fifteen months to make, and then had to be transported to Mexico and erected on site. In addition, he produced ceramics, enamels and jewellery.

Tiffany exhibited all over the world. He was awarded the French *Légion d'Honneur*, Gold Medals in Paris, St. Petersburg, Dresden, Buffalo, St. Louis, San Francisco and Philadelphia, a Grand Prix in Turin in 1902, and another in Seattle. In 1902 he changed the company name to Tiffany Studios. Early in his endeavours Tiffany wanted a trade name for his products. Nash suggested *Fabrile*, an Old English word meaning 'handmade', but Tiffany soon changed it to *Favrile,* which was applied to the entire range of products, and was registered at the U.S. Patent Office in November 1894. On the death of his father, in 1902, he became vice-president and artistic director of Tiffany & Co.

Tiffany produced a wide range of tableware in opaque gold or blue iridescent glass in many different patterns. It includes every sort of drinking glass, decanters, bowls, dessert and ice cream plates, comports, épergnes, pin trays, finger bowls, salt cellars and flower vases. Ranges of free-form vases included the spectacular *Jack-in-the-Pulpit* vases in gold and in blue. *Lustre Decorated Wares* had coloured glass applied to the surface of the vessel and combed into patterns with metal hooks to form leaf or feather designs. Once lustred the applied decoration was highly iridescent in contrast with the body of the vessel. *Cypriote Glass* was made in direct imitation of ancient buried glass, and had a pitted surface, sometimes with exploded surface bubbles. Always in simple shapes in keeping with ancient glass, it was made by rolling the parison over a layer of the same crushed glass, then lustring it. *Lava Glass* simulated a volcanic eruption, the roughly textured surface contrasted with highly polished gold lumps of 'lava' made by putting bits of basalt or talc onto the parison. The shapes are always free-formed, sometimes grotesque, as though fashioned by the heat of the magma. *Floriform Vases* have a bowl representing a flower, onion or bud, in wine-glass shape or free-form curves or a pinched rim set on a long slender stem which may have one or more bulges, set into a circular, bombe foot, each part of which may be plain or decorated. This range was first made by Thomas Manderson, the first gaffer at Corona. *Goose Neck Vases* were made in imitation of Persian rosewater flasks. *Reactive Glass*, which is glass that changed colour when reheated at the kiln was used to produce mysterious-looking flowers, such as Morning Glory, inside thick-walled vessels with the decoration trapped between the layers, while other flowers, such a gladioli, narcissi, daffodils and crocus were made using *millefiori* canes grouped together and cut across as in paper-

49: Louis Comfort Tiffany

50: *LOUIS C. TIFFANY AND CO.* Favrile Cypriote *vase, c. 1900. H. 26.4, Marks* L.C. Tiffany Inc. Favrile N5368 *with original paper label with* LCT *monogram. Victor Arwas Collection, London;* **51**: *abcde LOUIS C. TIFFANY & CO.* Favrile *miniatures (a) Red vase with silver chevrons. H. 8.9, Marks* L.C. Tiffany Favrile 795B, 1907; *(b) Gold double gourd vase. H. 6.5, Marks* L.C.T. 6034A, 1906; *(c) Polished blue, green and yellow vase with black vertical stripes. H. 5.9, Marks* L.C.T. R441; *(d) Iridescent vase with pulled green and gold leaves. H. 7.1, Marks* L.C.T. 1859A *with original paper label* Tiffany Favrile Glass Registered Trade Mark *with* LCT *Monogram, 1905; (e) Green vase with vertical ribs and aventurine inclusions. H. 6, Marks* L.C.T. R662. *Victor Arwas Collection, London;* **52**: *LOUIS C. TIFFANY & CO.* Favrile *glass, c. 1900: left Vase in iridescent blue with gold swirls. H. 22.8, Marks* L.C.T. G246 Louis C. Tiffany; *right Pedestal bowl in iridescent gold, D.19, Marks* 1706 L.C. Tiffany Inc. Favrile. *Crafts Centre, Middlesbrough Borough Council.*

53

weights; these vases are sometimes called paperweight vases. *Tel El Amarna* vases were inspired by vessels found in the archaeological burial site of Amenhotep IV's capital in Egypt and consist of elegant shapes in undecorated matt lustre of various colours, such as green, brown, red or blue, with a linear zig-zag frieze of glass in a different colour, usually near the rim, over an iridescent ground. *Aquamarine Glass* was a small group of vases made in 1913 by Arthur E. Saunders, a gaffer sent by Tiffany to seek inspiration in Bermuda; it consisted of a very thick glass vessel, often green to look like water, decorated internally with water plants, seaweed or marine life, such as fish or sea urchins. A variant was a pond lily vessel, with lily pads seeming to float on the surface, their roots snaking down the vase.

Tiffany produced many variants, particularly finely wheel-carved vases using different glass surfaces, and some using *cameo* techniques. At the height of production, there were five glass shops in full production, the heat there being such that barrels of cold water were kept for the men to plunge their upper bodies in to cool off at frequent intervals.

In 1902 Tiffany bought a large estate at Oyster Bay, Long Island, where he built himself a house with eighty-four rooms and twenty-five bathrooms. Landscaping the 580 acres around the house cost over a million dollars. Lavishly decorated by his firm, the house also contained his various collections. The house and its collections were always open to his designers, who frequently accompanied him on his travels.

The entry of the United States into the First World War in 1916 led to very restricted production, as many of his men went to the front or into war work. By the end of the war he was seventy years old. He set up the Louis Comfort Tiffany Foundation to aid young artists. His credo was the worship of Beauty, and he firmly believed that exposure to his home and its contents was the finest introduction to art. Students had to be recommended by their art schools or established artists, and submit their work to a committee. Once admitted, they lived on the estate, where the stables and carriage houses had been adapted as living quarters and studios, and had the freedom of the house, the library, the tennis courts and bowling alleys. There was no formal instruction, as the students were supposed to be advanced enough to produce their own work, but visiting artists were always available to give advice. In 1920 he split the company into Tiffany Studios and the Louis C. Tiffany Furnaces Inc., keeping one share of the stock in Tiffany Furnaces, giving 110 shares to the Foundation, five to his son Charles who had joined Tiffany & Co., fifty-five to the Nashes, one to George F. Heidt, formerly of the Heidt family glassworks but now a director of Tiffany & Co. and a member of the Board of Trustees of the Foundation, and eight to Joseph Briggs, the manager of Tiffany Studios.

Tiffany Studios ceased producing new designs, but went on assembling leaded glass windows, and, especially, leaded glass shades to fit stock bases. Joseph Briggs, who came from Accrington, in Lancashire, visited his home town and presented it with a superb collection of Tiffany glass, mosaics, tiles and other items, which are now on display in the Haworth Art Gallery there. Tiffany Studios had enormous stocks of glass and metal, and Briggs went on producing and selling lamps until his death in 1938, although the Company had to go into liquidation, and the contents had to be sold very cheaply in bulk.

Tiffany himself had become a lonely old man, his only companion a young Irish girl. He was out of sympathy

53: *LOUIS C. TIFFANY AND CO. Iridescent gold* Favrile *scarab seal, c. 1900. H. 4.5, Marks* LCT. *Iridescent glass scarab jewellery ornaments, c.1900. Length left 2, right 1.5. Victor Arwas Collection, London;* **54**: *Max Ritter von Spaun as a reserve officer*

with modern art, did not appreciate the work of the students of the Foundation, most of whom treated his creations with contempt. Tiffany Furnaces, run by A. Douglas Nash, created successful new lines but Tiffany himself resented the continued commercialisation of his name, transferred the remaining stock of vessels to Joseph Briggs, and closed down the Corona works, which he sold to Nash with the proviso that his name was not to be used. In January, 1933 Tiffany died. After the Second World War the Oyster Bay estate was stripped and its contents sold at auction for a fraction of their cost. The estate itself was broken up and sold in sections. In 1957 the house was destroyed by fire.

Iridescent glass was produced by several other American glassworks, including Steuben, Quezal (founded by a former Tiffany gaffer), Fostoria, Fenton, Lustre Art, Kew Blas and Durand. But Tiffany's most successful rival was the Bohemian firm of Loetz. Loetz was often accused of just copying Tiffany but a direct comparison of their product clearly shows two completely different aesthetic and scientific approaches. Loetz did, very occasionally, produce a Tiffany-style design with the laudable ambition of competing with the American giant at a lower price, but then Tiffany, too, occasionally produced a Loetz-style design with the equally laudable ambition of destroying his rival. Fortunately neither succeeded, and both produced a seemingly endless variety of shapes and colours.

JOHANN LOETZ (1778-1848) purchased, in 1840, a glassworks founded four years earlier by Johann B. Eisner von Eisenstein in Klostermühle. This was in Bohemia, the industrial centre of the Austro-Hungarian Empire that was also the home of some of the wealthiest and most aristocratic families in the Empire, because of its convenient location between Vienna, Prague and

54

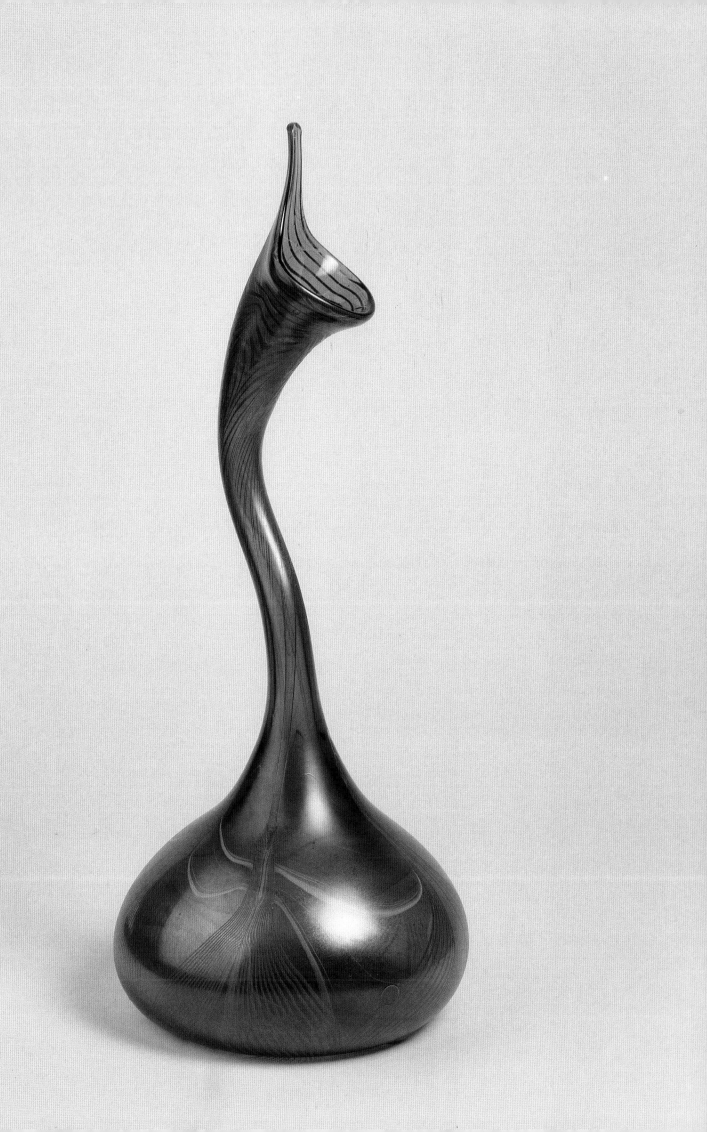

56

55: *LOUIS C. TIFFANY AND CO.* Favrile *goose-neck vase in green iridescent glass with drawn thread design in red, blue and cream, 1896. H. 40, Mark +1279. Courtesy of the Trustees of the V. & A.;* **56**: *LOUIS C. TIFFANY AND CO. Three floriform* Favrile *vases in iridescent glass, c. 1900: left H. 29.9, Marks L.C.T. 30A; centre H. 47.9, Marks L.C.T. N7504; right H. 38.7, Marks L.C.T. 2235A. Victor Arwas Collection, London*

57

Budapest, and because of its pastoral beauty, mountainous terrain and plentiful game for hunting. In 1848 Suzanne Loetz (1809-1899), his widow, took control of the firm, renaming it the Glasfabrik Johann Loetz-Witwe (the Widow Johann Loetz Glassworks). Her second husband was Dr. Franz Gerstner, a lawyer, but she was again widowed. She had had four children from her first marriage, but of the three boys one had died young, and only the younger Anton (1838-1877) came to work at the factory, becoming his mother's closest aide, but he, too, predeceased her. Her daughter Karoline married a lawyer, Maximilian Josef Anton Ritter von Spaun (Ritter is a German title equivalent to Knight, and was hereditary), son of an Imperial and Royal District Commissioner. The eldest of their three children, Max, frequently spent his holidays working at the glassworks, and his grandmother sent him to the technical university and then to Munich where he studied mechanical engineering for two years. In 1879 she put him in charge of running the glassworks.

MAX RITTER VON SPAUN modernised and expanded the glassworks and in 1879 appointed Eduard Prochazka manager in charge of production where he remained until 1914. In 1888 Spaun exhibited his first glass in imitation of hardstone at the Munich National Arts and Crafts Exhibition, and was awarded a Diploma, then a Grand Prix at the 1889 Paris International Exhibition where he displayed his hardstone glass in imitation of onyx, cornelian, agate, chalcedony, jasper and aventurine. He constantly introduced new designs, usually at international exhibitions, and concentrated increasingly on producing strongly coloured, patterned iridescent glass, taking out patents in 1895 and 1898.

In 1899 Spaun introduced his *Papillon* and *Phenomenon* ranges in Paris. *Papillon* (Butterfly) glass was opaque, flecked with multiple, closely clustered iridescent spots of raindrop shapes designed to look like a section of a butterfly's wing. *Phenomenon* glass was also iridescent, decorated with glass threads pulled at random across its surface. Both were produced in a variety of colours including Ruby (red), Candia (gold), Cobalt (blue). *Silberiris* was a textured glass surface with tiny pitting, used plain or with a chain design or in conjunction with other techniques. Spaun was awarded a Grand Prix in Paris at the 1900 Universal Exhibition. Loetz was, by then, one of the largest and most successful glassworks in Europe, with distributors in Vienna, Paris, Berlin, Hamburg, London and Madrid.

Although Spaun continued to design most of Loetz's production, his Vienna distributors, E. Bakalowits & Söhne, commissioned a number of designs for their retail shop, including several vases by professor Rudolf Bakalowits of Graz designed to perch on bronze mounts, and others by Koloman Moser and his students, in particular Robert Holubetz. Other members of the Wiener Werkstätte to design for Loetz included Josef Hoffmann (1870-1956), Otto Prutscher (1880-1949), Michael Powolny (1871-1954) and Dagobert Peche (1887-1923). Hans Bolek, Arnold Nechansky, Milla Weltmann, Leopold Bauer, Franz Hofstätter, Carl Witzmann and Marie Wilfert-Waltl also designed for Loetz, as did Eduard Prochazka and Maria Kirschner (1852-1931) who worked for Loetz from 1903 to 1914.

In addition to iridescent glass and its variants, Loetz introduced a range of cased vases, acid-etched in cameo in the style of industrial Gallé glass. While much of it is uninteresting, there were some vases that were both highly successful and original. These were signed with a variation of the Loetz signature in cameo. Another range of *cameo* vases, many in blue over red glass, signed *Richard*, were made expressly for the Paris firm of Edmond Etling.

Most of Loetz's iridescent glass was unsigned, signatures being reserved for pieces that were given or sold to museums and for pieces intended for export to countries requiring that imported goods give the country of origin, primarily the United States and, on occasion, Britain. These vases are normally marked *Loetz Austria* or *Austria* or *Austria* with crossed arrows, which were part of one of the Spaun coats of arms. These marks are on the base of the vase, which invariably has a polished pontil that can vary in size from quite small to almost the full size of the base. Museum examples in Austria and Germany normally spell the name *Lötz* and occasionally have the name of the designer. The Vienna firm of J. & L. Lobmeyr also commissioned considerable amounts of glass to their designs from Loetz.

A number of Loetz iridescent vases incorporate an overlaid design in silver or silver plate, sometimes with glass cabochons set into the metal, while others are inset in often elaborate brass or other metal mounts. Loetz shades were also made to fit bronze lamps by Gustav Gurschner, Peter Behrens, and other designers. Tsar Nicholas II had a number of Loetz lamps mounted in silver by Fabergé for use on his yacht.

In 1908, one year before his death, Max Ritter von Spaun transferred the Loetz glassworks to his eldest son, also named Max. The iridescent glass was now produced with a newly shiny surface, often with a pearly glaze, while curious sculptural creations emerged from the factory: twisted polychrome flower forms, but also cats, rabbits, penguins, elephants and other animals. Orange, pink, black and other 'modern' colours appeared in vases with rims in contrasting colours or with geometric decoration. In 1911 the company became

58

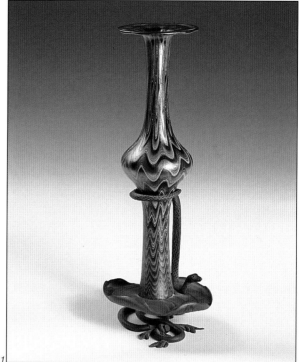

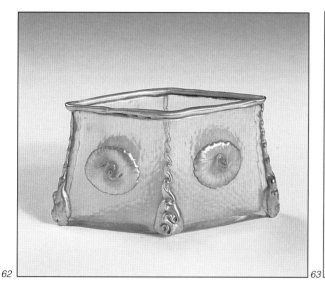

59: LOETZ (Glasfabrik Johann Loetz-Witwe) Vase in clear glass cased in orange and red-purple and acid-etched with a floral design probably by Josef Hoffmann, c. 1920. H.16.4, Mark Loetz and 12730. Courtesy of the Trustees of the National Museums of Scotland; *60*: LOETZ (Glasfabrik Johann Loetz-Witwe) Waisted metallic yellow Phenomenon vase, the G re2/ 514 decoration a variant of the Argus pattern, 1902. H. 21.3. Victor Arwas Collection, London; *61*: LOETZ (Glasfabrik Johann Loetz-Witwe) Creta Phenomenon vase in bronze snake mount, designed by Professor Rudolf Bakalowits in Graz and executed for the firm of E. Bakalowits & Söhne in Vienna, 1899. H. 33.4. Victor Arwas Collection, London; *62*: LOETZ (Glasfabrik Johann Loetz-Witwe), Nautilus vase in Candia Martelé glass, 1903. H. 8.6. Victor Arwas Collection, London; *63*: LOETZ (Glasfabrik Johann Loetz-Witwe) Vase in green and pale mauve/pink with applied metallic foil decoration, designed by Koloman Moser for retail by E. Bakalowits & Söhne, c. 1900. H.11.1. This vase was purchased from Liberty and Co. in 1902. The Manchester Metropolitan University

64

insolvent but was reorganised as a limited company in 1913. In 1918, at the end of the war, Austria had been dismembered, and Bohemia incorporated into the new country of Czechoslovakia, which with the various Bohemian industries was listed as the tenth richest country in the world. Klostermühle was now Klasterske Mlyn. Guillaume Janneau, writing in 1931, found that in Czechoslovakia, mostly in Bohemia, there were 148 glassworks, a further 29 providing raw glass, 4000 factories and home workshops engaged in glass decoration employing 30,000 glassblowers, as many glassworkers, and 90,000 glass decorators. Many of these turned out glass beads, bangles and buckles, and such oddities as spun glass curtains, blinds and dresses. Loetz continued the production of iridescent glass and vases with combed decoration, produced large quantities of acid-etched *cameo* glass, and crystal vases and bowls flashed with coloured crystal and cut in geometric shapes. Although the glassworks caught fire in 1930, sporadic production was resumed, and there is evidence that some glass was still being produced there as late as 1947 or 1948.

Two of the most successful Bohemian glassworks in competition with Loetz at the turn of the century were Meyr's Neffe and L. Moser & Söhne. MEYR'S NEFFE (Meyr's Nephews) was an amalgam of various glassworks brought together and split at various times by the descendants of Josef Meyr including his grandson, his nephews and their children. Meyr's surviving nephew, Wilhelm Kralik, left the company to his four sons. Two of the brothers took over two glassworks and renamed them Wilhelm Kralik Sohn; the two other brothers, Karl and Jugo Kralik, took over three glassworks and kept the name Meyr's Neffe, supplying the Vienna firm of J. & L. Lobmeyr with raw glass and running an engraving

and decorating workshop. At the 1873 Vienna International Exhibition Meyr's Neffe and Lobmeyr jointly exhibited iridescent glass. Meyr's Neffe made copies of old Bohemian glass as well as enamelled and gilt vases in Moorish style that were exhibited in Paris at the 1900 Universal Exhibition. It later executed vases, bowls and beakers designed by Koloman Moser and Josef Olbrich for E. Bakalowits & Söhne. From 1922 the firm executed designs by Otto Prutscher, Josef Hoffmann and Koloman Moser, as well as other members of the Secessionist Wiener Werkstätte.

Ludwig Moser & Söhne was founded in Karlsbad, a world famous spa, in 1857 by LUDWIG MOSER (1833-1916) as a workshop providing a glass polishing and engraving service for North Bohemian designers. He engraved goblets, dressing-table items and trinkets which proved very popular with visitors to the spa town. He was awarded a medal at the 1873 Vienna International Exhibition and was granted an Imperial warrant to supply the Court. As he expanded, he took on a number of designers, including Johann Hoffmann (1840-1922), Josef Urban (1827-1895) and his son Julius, and Rudolf Hiller (1827-1915) and his son. In 1893 he took over the glassworks at Meierhofen, thus creating a completely integrated factory that was registered as Karlsbaderglasindustrie Gesellschaft Ludwig Moser & Söhne. He and his sons Rudolf and Gustav employed four hundred workers.

Moser's designs included a large number of opaque dark blue or black vases and bowls moulded in geometric facets, their wide frieze sand-blasted with a classical scene in shallow relief and gilt. Most of these, and the opaque blue, black or purple objects moulded with figures of nude women or animals were designed by Johann Hoffmann, and are usually signed with his name or unsigned. Transparent iridescent vases enamelled and gilt with Classical or Ancient Egyptian motifs; vases in clear glass enamelled and gilt with complex naturalistic scenes of birds or animals with plants and foliage; faceted clear or coloured vessels with heavily gilt panels shallow carved with genre scenes; blow moulded vases deeply incised with flowers, padded with brightly coloured glass; *cameo* glass in the style of late industrial Gallé - all these and more were made at the Moser works, but their most attractive glass consisted of transparent vases, colourless except at the base, padded at various places on the surface with blobs of opaque coloured glass that were wheel-carved as intricate flowerheads, with the stems and leaves deeply wheel-carved in *intaglio*.

Moser exhibited in the International Exhibitions in Paris in 1878 and 1900 (Silver Medal), Brussels in 1897, Turin in 1902, the Austrian Arts & Crafts in London, 1902, Liège in 1905 and the German Bohemian in 1906 (Diploma). At the end of the First World War Karlsbad became Karlovy Vary. In the 1920s Moser executed designs for members of the Wiener Werkstätte, including Josef Hoffmann, Hilda Jesser, E.J. Wimmer, Dagobert Peche and Julius Zimpel. In 1922, under the direction of Leo and Richard Moser, the firm took over its greatest rival, Meyr's Neffe.

65

68

66: *LOETZ (Glasfabrik Johann Loetz-Witwe)* Creta Pampas *vase, executed for the firm of Tschernich & Co. Haida, 1899. H. 30.3. Bristol Museums and Art Gallery;* **67**: *Possibly by LUDWIG MOSER & SÖHNE Vase in shaded green glass with engraved iris, c. 1905. H. 28, Mark CFT monogram. Broadfield House Glass Museum, Kingswinford;* **68**: *LUDWIG MOSER & SÖHNE Pedestal bowl, acid-etched and gilt with frieze of classical figures, c. 1900. D. 18. Broadfield House Glass Museum, Kingswinford*

PATE DE VERRE

Pâte de verre was a type of glass made by packing a refractory mould with powdered fragments of coloured glass mixed with a binding agent to make a paste, then placing this into a muffle furnace, similar to that used in the production of ceramics, for extended periods at relatively low temperature until it vitrified. The mould could be removed at various stages, and the composition retouched before vitrification. The different colours could be kept separate, unlike normal glassmaking when colours would run into each other in the heat of the kiln. The process of annealing was also very long and slow. This type of moulded glass was known to the ancient Egyptians and in classical Greece and Rome, but the technique had been lost.

HENRI CROS (1840-1907) was born in Narbonne into an extremely well-educated and intellectually active family. His grandfather had translated the *Idylls* of Theocritus into French, had written textbooks, and taught literature. His father had studied law and taught philosophy, on which he had published two books, but his vehemently expressed Republicanism and Socialism meant he was frequently out of work. Henri Cros, who was proficient in Greek and Latin and had taught himself some Hebrew, decided on a career in art, and studied sculpture with François Jouffroy and painting with Jules-Emmanuel Valadon and Louis-Jules Etex. He first exhibited a plaster bust at the 1861 Paris Salon and later experimented with portrait busts in bronze, plaster, terracotta, alabaster and marble. In a desire to sculpt polychrome figures, he began to exhibit statues in coloured wax, receiving several commissions. He also experimented with encaustic painting, publishing a book on the technique.

Close examination of some of the glass plaques in the Louvre Museum convinced him that they could not have been executed traditionally in a kiln, and he began a long and detailed period of research into recreating the techniques used. In 1884 he created his first glass paste medallion, a portrait of his niece, in the oven in his kitchen, though he later built himself a kiln in his workshop. From then on he devoted himself increasingly to working with pâte de verre, using it to produce plaques, roundels and medallions with relief decoration of archaic and classical subjects, often giving it a rough surface or broken edges to increase the look of antiquity.

Cros was awarded a Silver Medal at the 1869 International Exhibition in Paris, and his pâte-de-verre plaques so impressed the Director of the Ecole des Beaux-Arts that he recommended that the Manufacture Nationale de Sèvres put a kiln at his disposal. The administration at Sèvres was reluctant to do so but the Director's successor, Henri Roujon, obtained a ministerial order in 1891, and finally persuaded Sèvres to give Cros a spare kiln in 1893; he also persuaded the Fine Arts Ministry to give Cros a grant. Cros began experimenting with larger panels, which had to be made in sections that were later assembled; the first one - *The Story of Water* - was completed in 1894. The following year he was decorated with the *Légion d'Honneur*. A workshop was finally found for him in a disused windmill at Sèvres, and construction begun on a new large kiln, which was completed in 1897. He could now execute the monumental pâte-de-verre panels he had planned. His second major panel - *The Story of Fire* - was completed in 1900, shown at the Paris Universal Exhibition, and won him a Gold Medal. It was purchased for the Museum of Decorative Arts in Paris. His third major panel - *The Apotheosis of Victor Hugo* - was completed in 1905, and installed in Hugo's house, which is now a museum. His last major panel was to be a huge overmantel for the

Prince de Wagram's castle at Grosvois, but his death in 1907 interrupted the project. A very secretive artist he only revealed his techniques to his son JEAN CROS (1884-1932), the only one of his three children to work with him. Jean completed the overmantel and continued to work in his father's studio, executing a series of plaques of Provençal landscapes and other scenes inspired by the *Nabis* painters. He also cast several *pâte-de-verre* models after sculpture by his friends Antoine Bourdelle and Auguste Rodin. He was served with a notice to quit by Sèvres in 1912, and set up a studio in his home. From 1918 until his death he specialised in making *pâte-de-verre* plaques for wall lights and lamps, helped by his younger sister. He never revealed his father's secrets, which died with him.

Unknown to each other, Henri Cros's researches into recreating *pâte de verre* were paralleled by those of GEORGES DESPRET (1862-1952). Born in Belgium, he had inherited the Glaceries de Jeumont, a small glassworks in France, from his uncle. He soon expanded the works, took over two more glassworks, and manufactured a wide range of mirrors, glass wall cladding, tiles and plate glass, and soon began to experiment with *pâte de verre*. It took him more than ten years of constant experimentation to devise an appropriate binding agent and a paste that did not break down or crack during vitrification. He exhibited these at the 1900 Universal Exhibition in Paris, and many were purchased by the Museum of Decorative Arts in Paris and the Museum of Applied Arts in Berlin. He executed several copies of Tanagra figurines in the Louvre, but soon employed a number of sculptors, including Georges Nicollet, Charles Troche, M. de Glori, Jean Goujon, Alexandre Charpentier, Yvonne Serruys and Pierre Le Faguays to design for him.

He produced a number of masks in a single colour and polychrome; the earlier ones involved multiple firings, one for each colour, the later ones a single firing for all colours simultaneously. The largest was a portrait of Cléo de Mérode, a ballet dancer and great beauty. He also created vases and bowls that looked like carved hardstones or marble, others that resembled Oriental pottery. But much of his production was sculptural, achieving an opaque quality that reflects light with apparent translucence, and a range of both subtle and solid colours. He exhibited his pâte de verre regularly at the Salons of the Société Nationale des Beaux-Arts from 1900, at the 1908 Franco-British Exhibition in London, the 1910 Artistic Glass and Crystal Exhibition in Paris, and the 1911 International Exhibition in Turin. Despret's Glassworks was destroyed during the First World War, as was the collection of his finest pieces and all the documentation he had given to the Jeumont Communal Museum, which was also bombed. He reopened the works in 1920 with a very reduced output, had a last major exhibition in Liège in Belgium in 1930, and finally closed down in 1937, dying shortly after his ninetieth birthday.

FRANCOIS DECORCHEMENT (1880-1971) was born in Conches, in Normandy, into a family of artists and artisans. His father, a professor of sculpture at the Ecole Nationale des Arts Décoratifs, had executed a number of sculptures for the painter Léon Gérome. François graduated from the Ecole des Arts Décoratifs in 1900, began to paint and potted some stoneware. At his father's suggestion, he began to experiment with *pâte d'émail*, so-called enamel paste, which had been exhibited by ALBERT DAMMOUSE (1848-1926), a ceramist who had worked in Limoges and especially for Charles Haviland at Auteuil, before setting up a work-

70

71

69: *GEORGES DESPRET Pedestal dish in* pâte de verre, *representing the Three Graces holding up a sea-shell with green and orange highlights imitating mother-of-pearl, with the base showing children blowing conch shells, designed by the sculptor Yvonne Serruys, c.1926. H. 40, Marks Despret 940. Robert Zehil, Private Collection, Monaco;* **70**: *GEORGES DESPRET* Pâte de verre: *left Relief model of a woman's head, purple, H. 10.8, Mark G. Despret; centre Relief polychrome model of a man's head, H. 15.8, Marks G. Despret; right Relief model of a baby's pink head, H. 8.5, Mark G. Despret. All c. 1905. Victor Arwas Collection, London;* **71**: *HENRI CROS* Pâte de verre *relief polychrome models of archaic women's heads, c.1910. H. left 9.1, right 9.5. Victor Arwas Collection, London*

shop at Sèvres. During the 1890s he experimented with glass paste, producing a very thin, delicate, translucent material that was dubbed *pâte d'émail*, and was frequently thought to be some form of ceramic, not glass.

Décorchement did not start with powdered glass, but made his own raw glass from silicates mixed with lead or metallic oxides to obtain crystal, coloured or opal glass, which was then pulverised. He used quince pips as a binding agent. Delicate and friable, little of this early *pâte d'émail* survived the process of vitrification. Based on Art Nouveau designs, frequently floral, they were sometimes modelled with open cloisons that were occasionally filled with translucent enamels and refired. Exhibiting at the Salons of the Société des Artistes Français he was awarded an Honourable Travelling Scholarship in 1908. On his return he moved back to his native Conches, set up a petroleum-fired kiln, and produced a new type of vase. This time he used the lost wax method of reproducing his designs, and used higher temperatures to produce a crystalline, translucent material which he then polished to a very shiny finish. This was dubbed *pâte de cristal*, although, like *pâte d'émail* it is only a variant of *pâte de verre*. He was awarded a Gold Medal for it at the 1911 Salon.

The First World War interrupted his production, and for the first two years after his return he continued to produce basically Art Nouveau designs, increasingly simplifying both shape and decoration through the 1920s, using more abstract and geometric patterns. His works were on permanent exhibition in Geo. Rouard's store. The 1925 Paris Exhibition was very successful for him, and he was elected a Full Member of the Société des Artistes Français and the Salon d'Automne, and a Committee Member of the Salon des Artistes Décorateurs. He exhibited at most of the major International Exhibitions throughout the world, and received the *Légion d'Honneur* in 1926. From about 1925 onwards Décorchement increasingly abandoned surface decoration for more chunky geometric shapes and bright sharp colours, such as pinks and acid greens. In the 1930s he spent much time developing new types of Church windows, using *pâte de verre* instead of glass, and cement instead of leading. He returned to *pâte de verre* production after the Second World War; making his last vessel a month before he died at the age of ninety-one.

JOSEPH-GABRIEL ROUSSEAU (1885-1953) was born in Meslay-le-Vidame, a small village in the Eure-et-Loire. His family were all farm-workers, but he won a scholarship enabling him to complete secondary school and, aged 17, he was admitted to the National High School for Ceramics at Sèvres. Jean Cros was a fellow student, and he was thus introduced to Henri Cros, who was working in his studio at Sèvres. In 1906 he graduated, and was appointed manager of a small ceramics research laboratory. He also opened a small workshop of his own, and began to manufacture porcelain teeth. In 1913 he married the sister of a fellow pupil at Sèvres. She was the daughter of a celebrated Greek-born lawyer, Panagiotis Argyriades. On his marriage he adopted part of his wife's surname, and was henceforth known as GABRIEL ARGY-ROUSSEAU. A year later he exhibited his first pâte-de-verre designs at the Salon of the Société des Artistes Français. When war was declared he joined up as a national defence engineer, and carried out research in various scientific fields, including photography, which enabled him over the years to take out a number of patents from which he managed to eke an existence in old age when his glass creations went out of favour. In 1919 he designed and manufactured a range of clear glass scent bottles enamelled with flowers, butterflies and pretty maidens for the firm of Marcel Franck and others. Gustave-Gaston Moser-Millot, the owner of a major decorative art gallery on the Boulevard des Italiens (it still exists), who represented a number of Bohemian firms, was so impressed by Argy-Rousseau's designs that he set up a limited company in 1921, Les Pâtes de Verre d'Argy-Rousseau, with himself as principal shareholder and Chairman, and Argy-Rousseau as Managing Director. The invested capital was enough to open a comfortable workshop employing several dozen workers and decorators. The designs were sold in the Moser-Millot gallery.

Argy-Rousseau could now concentrate on design and technical perfection. He developed an astonishing range of translucent colours, including very rich reds, purples and greens which were particularly successful in shades for table lights, ceiling fittings and night-lights. He designed an exceptionally popular range of vases with animals, lions, wolves, deer, and butterflies. A vase with a shoal of angel fish swimming into and out of stylised waves enabled him to show the subtle gradations of colour as the fish were partly concealed by the waves. The same models were produced in different combinations of colours. Another attractive range consisted of female nudes and dancers as well as classical historical and mythological figures and masks. In the mid 1920s his designs became increasingly abstract and geometric, and in some cases his vases were identical to Décorchement's, although it would be impossible to work out which came first. He also produced a range of *pâte-de-verre* pendants with flowers, animals and insects.

In 1925 he was appointed a member of the Jury for Glass at the International Exhibition. Three years later the sculptor Marcel Bouraine designed a series of female figures and an indoor fountain which Argy-Rousseau executed in several brilliant colours in *pâte de cristal*. Following the New York Stock Market crash of 1929 Moser-Millot dissolved the Company without consulting Argy-Rousseau, who suddenly found himself unemployed. Without a proper workshop, he executed some enamelled vessels and simple designs, accepting orders for a few religious plaques. After the Second World War his only revenue was from the meagre royalties from his patents.

Unlike the other *pâte-de-verre* artists Argy-Rousseau wrote detailed reports on his techniques, including temperatures, time in the kiln and time in the lehr, the composition of the paste, the manufacture of the sectional mould, and the techniques and materials used in the final polishing. He used powdered glass much of the time to create true pâte de verre, although he also used powdered lead crystal to make *pâte de cristal*. With a number of workers, a semi-industrial production process and the right equipment, he was able to ensure that every piece that came out of his workshop was as perfect as possible and had been made using the correct technique. Independent *pâte-de-verre* artists tended to take shortcuts: they used powdered crystal much of the time because the higher the lead content, the lower the temperature needed for vitrification.

When the *pâte-de-verre* creators of the early part of the twentieth century were rediscovered, several writers considered Décorchement superior to Argy-Rousseau because he was a sole artist. In fact both were amazingly creative, although Argy-Rousseau may have the edge for his adventurous choice of subjects.

AMALRIC WALTER (1870-1959) was born in Sèvres where both his father and grandfather had been porcelain decorators; he attended the Manufacture's National School before being apprenticed there. Inspired by the work of Henri Cros and Albert Dammouse, he began to experiment with *pâte de verre* in association with one of his former teachers, Gabriel Lévy. They exhibited their first joint production at the 1903 Salon of the Société Nationale des Beaux-Arts: small vases, a tray and a couple of sculptures after Denys Puech and Eugène Delagrange. Antonin Daum, interested in new techniques for his expanding glassworks in Nancy, offered Walter and Lévy a workshop. They were to execute a stated number of vases, bowls, shades and decorative panels, some to their own designs, others to designs by Daum, after which Daum was to pay them an agreed sum and acquire the rights to their technique. Lévy did not agree, and his partnership with Walter was dissolved. Walter remained and continued to work at Daum. His early work was almost colourless, but adapting the Daum technique of applying coloured glass powder to both the surface of the item to be vitrified and to the inside of the mould remedied the problem. Daum supplied Walter with museum copies of Tanagra figurines, Victor Prouvé supplied him with a statue of the American dancer Loïe Fuller, and finally HENRI BERGE (1868-1936), Daum's chief decorator and head teacher of Daum's school of decoration, began supplying him with a wide selection of designs, mostly of small animals. Walter's first production at Daum was a massive panel with grapes in relief. Other panels followed, designed to stand independently in a carved wood support made by Majorelle, or were designed to fit into Majorelle furniture, while a spectacular table jardinière in metal was designed to incorporate panels on all sides. In addition to the relief panels there were smooth panels with a landscape incorporated in the surface. Many of the panels cracked or split during the making. All are now exceedingly rare.

The *pâte de verre* workshop was closed down at the outbreak of war in 1914. After the Armistice Walter decided to open his works independently. He was allowed to carry on making the prewar designs, and Bergé went on designing for him in his spare time for the rest of his life. Walter also came to an agreement with the ceramics factory of Mougin Frères, which gave him access to all their sculptors and designs. Selling through a network of expensive jewellers and gold and silver smiths, things went well for him until the death of Bergé, who had become a great friend. He realised at the same time that the vogue for *pâte de verre* was passing, that his designs did not conform with the taste for geometric Art Deco, that sales were dwindling following the 1929 crash, and that his sight was failing. He sought more, and cheaper outlets, produced smaller and cheaper models, which were to be found in stationers and ironmongers and, like Argy-Rousseau, executed simple religious plaques. Very little *pâte de verre* was made between 1935 and 1940, when he took refuge in the country. When the war was over he worked with one man until the man's death in the fifties and his own complete blindness. He died among friends in 1959, completely forgotten.

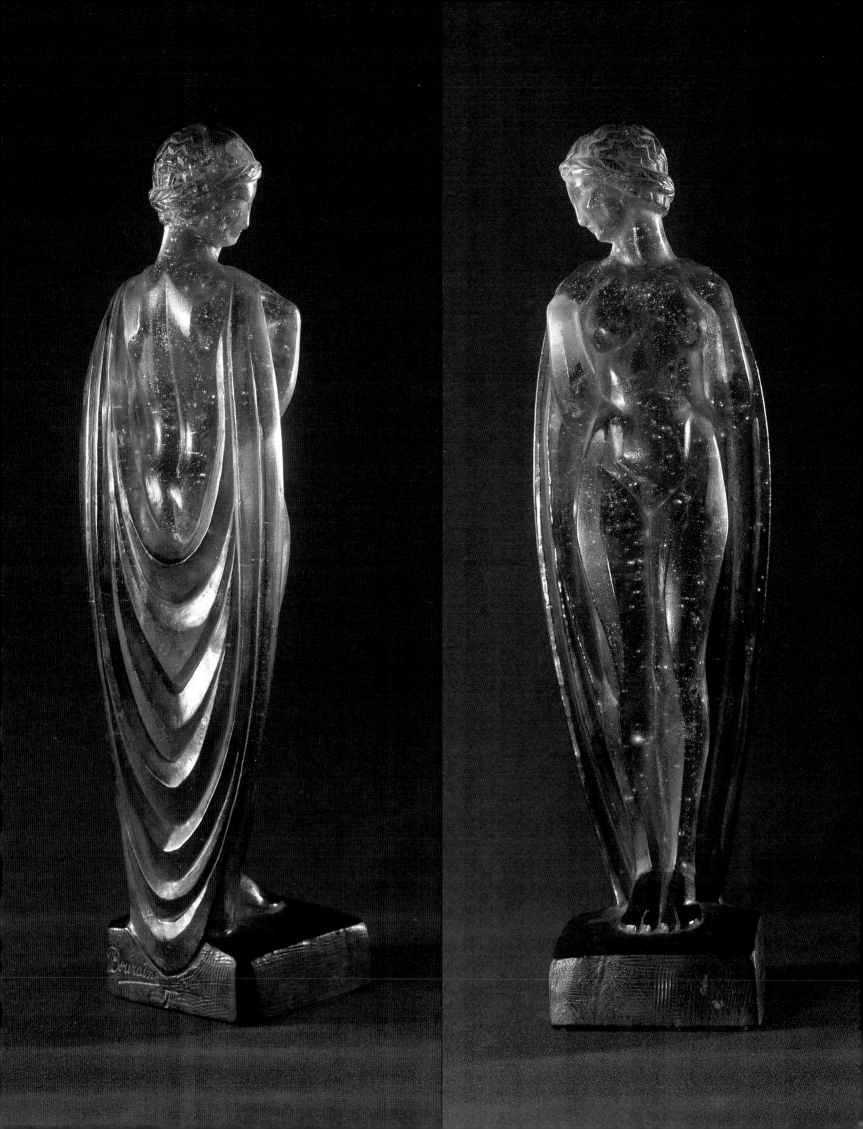

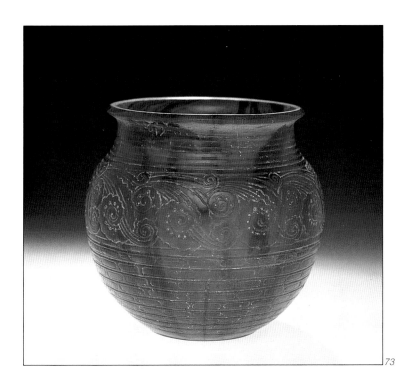

73

72: JOSEPH-GABRIEL ARGY-ROUSSEAU Pâte de verre *statuette* Jeunesse *in blue-mauve, the model designed by Marcel Bouraine, c. 1928. H. 28, Marks* Argy-Rousseau *and* Bouraine. *United Group International SA, courtesy of Galerie Moderne, London;* **73**: *FRANÇOIS-EMILE DECORCHEMENT Bulbous blue* pâte de cristal *vase with black tints, decorated with stylised moulded flowers, c.1923-24. H. 23, Marks* Decorchement *in a horseshoe and* C760. *Robert Zehil, Private Collection, Monaco;* **74**: *ALMERIC WALTER* Pâte de verre *tray modelled with a fish, c.1920. W. 25.5 , Marks* A. Walter. *Private collection, courtesy of Colonel and Madame G. Ury (Galerie Moderne, London)*

74

ART DECO

PRESSED GLASS-FUNCTIONALISM

RENE LALIQUE (1860-1945) embarked on a new career at the age of fifty-eight. Born in Ay, in the Champagne district, he had been guided by his mother into a career in jewellery. By the turn of the century he had become the most celebrated jeweller in the world. Crowned heads, including Queen Alexandra, possessed his creations, and the biggest collection of his works, constituted by Calouste Gulbenkian ("Mr Five-per-cent", so-called because this represented his share of the exploitation of the oil wells of Iraq), is now the core of the Gulbenkian Foundation Museum in Lisbon. He was also a fine sculptor, executing works in bronze, ivory, silver and gold. He often incorporated ivory, horn and glass in his jewellery. The massive glass panels he designed for the front door of his new house in Paris were cast in the Saint Gobain glassworks.

In 1902 he rented a small workshop in Clairefontaine, near Rambouillet, equipped it, and hired four experienced glassworkers. Using the *cire perdue* or lost wax method of casting, he sculpted a series of small figurines and vases which were cast as unique examples. He later devised reusable moulds so that more than one cast could be made. In 1907 the perfumer Coty commissioned some scent-bottle labels from him. He ended up designing both labels and bottles, which were made at the Legras glassworks, and he became so fascinated with the process that he rented a small glassworks at Combs-la-Ville, not far from Paris.

Lalique ceased making precious jewellery in 1911. When the First World War ended in 1918, Alsace and the part of Lorraine annexed by Germany in 1870 were reinstated as part of France. Lalique purchased a large glassworks at Wingen-sur-Moder, close to the German border, and named it the Verrerie d'Alsace, putting his son Marc in charge of production. He was determined to produce fine quality glass using modern industrial techniques and mass production methods. Some of his glass was blown into moulds, but those vessels with more complex relief were produced in the stamping press, a technique he pioneered. Guillaume Janneau described it in his Modern Glass (1931): "The glassmaker's press is composed of two elements: the actual mould, consisting of two jaws, one of which is fixed, and the mandrel, controlled by a large lever. The operator collects a certain quantity of glass in a state of fission, which he allows to run into the mould. At the proper moment his assistant severs with shears the thick, glowing-red mass, then pulls down the lever as far as it will go. The mandrel is set in motion and pushes the molten glass into the jaws of the mould, which press it and shape it simultaneously from within and without, imprinting on the soft mass every detail of the decoration. This method, of course, cannot be used for closed vessels, and there is, too, a risk of breakage during the cooling process. There is also some difficulty in constructing anything on a large scale - statuary, for instance - the problem being to avoid the premature contraction of the cooling surface over a core that retains the heat." In René Lalique's opinion an operation of this kind would take several months.

Lalique produced an enormous quantity of new models with a demi-crystal of his own composition which was particularly malleable. He used clear, coloured and opalescent glass, as well as a surface patination of the shallow parts of the composition to increase the contrast with the prominent sections. Mould marks were eliminated during the final polishing, an important part of the manufacturing process.

Lighting, too, was important, and Lalique produced elaborate electroliers, table lamps, light bowls, lanterns,

75: René Lalique

76: Marius-Ernest Sabino

illuminated panels, wall lights, and moulded sections that could be joined up to form extended lit cornices. Complex fountains were designed for use in the street and within buildings. Extremely thin glass was used for drinking vessels, and massive glass for furniture such as cocktail cabinets, bars and illuminated dining and occasional tables. He also produced glass jewellery, pendants, rings, brooches, bracelets and bead necklaces; and a range of car mascots or bonnet or hood ornaments, many of which doubled as paperweights.

The 1925 Paris Exhibition was a triumph for the ubiquitous Lalique, who had devised a spectacular outdoor illuminated fountain, set up a complete pavilion for his products, designed the dining room of the Sèvres pavilion with an astonishing coffered glass illuminated ceiling in addition to the table, the lighting and the tableware, and had architectural or decorative items in several more pavilions. He supplied panels, lighting and other creations for the French liners, the *Paris* in 1920, the *Ile-de-France* in 1927 and the *Normandie* in 1935; installed a glass panel moulded with running figures above the doorway to the restaurant in Claridge's Hotel in London; provided the altar for the Convent of the Deliverance at Caen; and completely decorated the interior of St. Matthew's Church in St. Helier, Jersey, with moulded glass panels modelled with Madonna lilies in high relief. He exhibited regularly in various Salons and international exhibitions. Retrospective exhibitions of his work were held in Paris, in the Pavillon de Marsan (the Museum of Decorative Arts), in 1933 and again in 1991-1992. The Combs-la-Ville glassworks closed down in 1937 and Wingen-sur-Moder was occupied by the invading German forces who destroyed the equipment. In 1945 the factory was returned to Lalique shortly before he died. His son, Marc Lalique (1900-

1977), completely refitted the factory, but changed to the exclusive use of crystal with a high lead content. He reintroduced colour in the 1970s. He was succeeded by his daughter Marie-Claude Lalique (b. 1935) who reintroduced jewellery.

Opalescent glass was made in Europe as early as the 16th century. Different countries used different ingredients to achieve a milky shininess with a bluish tinge and internal golden reflections. French glassmakers traditionally used antimony or arsenic to achieve the milkiness with the addition of a trace of cobalt for the blue. In Bohemia they liked to use bone ash. The density of the opalescence was dependent on the speed with which the outside of the glass cooled by comparison with its centre: the thicker the glass, the greater the opalescence. The final touches involved washing the object in acid and polishing to a high gloss. Lalique was undoubtedly the most famous maker of opalescent glass, but there were others including Etling, Verlys, Pierre d'Avesn, André Hunebelle, Verlux, Val Saint Lambert's Luxval range, and Barolac in Bohemia. One of the best was MARIUS ERNEST SABINO (1878-1961), a Sicilian who became a naturalised Frenchman in 1914 and volunteered to join the French Army as a bombardier. Trained as a sculptor, he set up a large enterprise manufacturing a range of glass and metal lamps of all types, architectural glass fitments, and a wide range of clear, frosted, coloured and opalescent vases, bowls and figurines, all of which he designed himself. His opalescence was very rich and used a much higher percentage of arsenic than Lalique. He exhibited at various Salons and most International Exhibitions, receiving a large number of awards, including a Gold Medal for glass and a Silver Medal for metalwork at the 1925 Paris Exhibition, and the *Légion d'Honneur* in

77: *MAURICE MARINOT Clear glass footed cup, bubbled throughout, deeply acid-etched to form polished and slightly faceted lozenges, the neck and foot deeply etched in irregular facets. Florence Marinot, the artist's daughter has dated it 1934 in her Certificate. H. 31.5 cm, Mark marinot and Florence Marinot's label, numbered 2376. Formerly in the Collection of Adrien Hébrard, in whose gallery Marinot exhibited regularly. Robert Zehil, Private Collection, Monaco;* **78**: *ARISTIDE COLOTTE Blow-moulded clear crystal vase deeply wheel-carved with chevrons and cabochons, the irregular background patinated with old gold, the cabochons highly polished, c. 1930-35. H. 20.5, Marks Colotte Nancy Pièce Unique. Robert Zehil, Private Collection, Monaco;* **79**: *AUGUSTE HEILIGENSTEIN Transparent vase with an overall enamel design, a large band of intricately entwined stylised leaves with vertical bands above and below in green, emerald and brown, with a gold band at top and bottom, c. 1925. H.18, Mark aug. heiligenstein. Robert Zehil, Private Collection, Monaco*

80: *HENRI NAVARRE Transparent bubbled vase in the shape of a flower bud, applied with stylised leaves. H. 23, Marks,* H. Navarre 867. *Robert Zehil, Private Collection, Monaco;* **81**: *MARCEL GOUPY Clear glass vase enamelled all over on the inside surface with orange and externally with an African scene of hunters in a canoe chasing pink ibis in polychrome with gilding, c. 1925. H. 23, Mark* M. Goupy. *Robert Zehil, Private Collection, Monaco;* **82**: *JEAN LUCE Clear glass pedestal bowl decorated with stylised flowers and leaves in blue, white, grey and black enamels, c.1920. H.26, Mark JL monogram. Robert Zehil, Private Collection, Monaco*

83

84

1931. In order to compete with lower-priced opalescence, he launched two cheaper ranges under the trademarks *Verart* and *Vernox*. He stopped manufacturing in 1939, but his son produced a range of small figurines in the 1960s for export to the United States, but these were in a different, creamier, less translucent opalescence than those of the interwar years.

Two curious pressed glass vessels, a vase and a jug, were designed by GEORGES DE FEURE (1868-1943) in the 1930s. Symbolist painter, stage designer, poster and graphic artist, he had designed furniture, fans, cane-handles and silver for Bing's *L'Art Nouveau*; he also designed ceramics at Limoges, fabrics, stained glass and books. The jug had a rough surface; the vase was moulded in purple, grey, black or transparent glass with a frieze of Hellenic dancers. It was commissioned by the firm of Fauchon and was normally sold filled with chocolates or sugared almonds. Georges de Feure also designed two *cameo* vases, acid-etched with Hellenic scenes, which were executed at the Daum works.

Another opalescent glass manufacturer was James A. Jobling & Co. a Sunderland glassworks first established in 1858. Jobling put his nephew Ernest Purser as works manager and chief technologist in 1902, and he began a long modernisation programme. In 1924 Purser was named as his uncle's heir, and took the name Ernest Jobling-Purser. After the First World War he acquired the right to manufacture and market Pyrex glass in Britain and the Empire (except for Canada) from Corning in New York, and its plain, well-designed range was both admired and commercially successful. He also tried a line in coloured pressed glass, but this was unsuccessful. Pressed glass in Britain was traditionally a cheap substitute for cut crystal, and it was difficult to persuade the manufacturer or the buying public other-

wise. Jobling's approached Lalique in 1931 with an offer to manufacture his glass in England under licence on a royalty basis. Turned down by Lalique, Jobling's then approached Sabino, who evinced interest, but he was considered too expensive. Jobling's then purchased several pieces by Lalique and Sabino, analysed them, rejected Sabino's composition for excess arsenic, and opted for Lalique's with the firm intention of undercutting his prices for similar glass. English designers seemed unable to overcome their conviction that pressed glass should reproduce cut glass, so Jobling's purchased a number of Lalique-style designs from French designers and commissioned Etienne Franckhauser, mould-maker to many French glasshouses including Lalique, Sabino and Hunebelle, to make the necessary clay-shellacked and plaster models and bronze moulds. Lalique polished and occasionally wheel-carved all mould marks from the glass. Jobling's chose to fire-polish them instead, that is to put the vessel into the kiln at high temperature. While this saved on time and labour, and gave a high gloss to the surface, it also tended to blur the fine detail of the relief. Whether it was the designs, the quality of glass used, or the corner-cutting detail, Jobling's opalescent glass, which was called *Opalique*, though often charming, did not have the commanding presence of the products of Lalique, Sabino or Etling. Poor sales eventually ended the venture in around 1940.

Several other British manufacturers essayed coloured pressed glass vessels in fairly adventurous shapes, including Bagley & Co. of Knottingley in Yorkshire, who began the production of pressed flint glass in the 1920s, then introduced colours and new shapes in 1933 under the name of *Crystaltint*. They employed ALEXANDER H. WILLIAMSON of the Royal College of Art as an occa-

85

sional outside designer. Sowerby's Ellison Glass Works Ltd. of Gateshead, which produced a wide range of pressed coloured fancy glass as well as tableware, brought out *Carnival* glass and ruby-coloured vessels in 1926 and pastel-coloured shades in the early 1930s; and George Davidson and Co. Ltd. of the Teams Glass Works, Gateshead, produced simple pressed coloured glass shapes from the early 1920s, includingvessels with matt surfaces and such spectacular colours as opaque green and scarlet and black.

In parallel with the production of pressed and opalescent glass a group of solitary artists individually produced vessels which came to typify another aspect of Art Deco. MAURICE MARINOT (1882-1960) was both painter and glass artist. He exhibited a painting in the 1905 Salon d'Automne which situated him as one of the original Fauve artists, then discovered the beauty of glass in 1911 on a visit to a small glassworks run by his friends the Viard brothers. He began by designing vessels which he then enamelled. Given a bench, he would arrive daily during the lunch break and practise while the staff was away. Soon he was making the glass with the occasional help of a boy. He abandoned enamelling, and produced two basic styles, one a smooth-surfaced vessel in various shapes trapping colours and patterns within its very thick walls, the other equally thick-walled but with its surface deeply cut or etched in abstract patterns. His glass was acclaimed internationally. A review by Walter Pach of his 1932 exhibition in New York compared his glass to the paintings of Matisse and Derain and the sculpture of Rodin. He gave up working with glass in 1937 when the Viard glassworks closed down. During the Allied bombing that preceded the Liberation his studio was blown up, destroying some 2500 paintings, thousands of drawings

and much of his glass. His daughter has given examples of his glass to major museums throughout the world. André Derain wrote: "A glass by Marinot: I have never seen anything as beautiful which was at the same time so precious and so simple."

HENRI NAVARRE (1885-1971) was a disciple of Marinot. Trained as an architect, he studied sculpture, gold- and silver-smithing, and the technical side of leaded-glass and mosaic manufacture. He executed public statuary as well as private commissions, including a massive figure of Christ in moulded glass and a reredos for the *Ile-de-France* liner. Smaller statues and plaques were made in bronze, stone, marble and wood, and medals in silver, gold and bronze; he designed architectural glass panels and windows. Inspired by Marinot, he designed thick-walled glasses in simple shapes, though occasionally more complex ones; they were generally pressed and internally decorated with intricate patterns, swirls of colour and strange granulations and textures. He also made several glass sculptures, including some abstracted portraits.

ARISTIDE COLOTTE (1885-1959) joined the Baccarat glassworks as a young boy. In 1925 he went to work for the Cristalleries de Nancy, set up as a rival of the Daum works, leaving a year later to set up on his own after receiving the first of two medals as Best Worker of France. Ordering large, heavy blocks of glass from Baccarat, he would etch, carve, chisel and file them into transparent sculpture. A bust of the *Sorrowing Christ*, carved from a 500lb block is now in the Vatican Museum, and he exhibited a massive figure of a dolphin carved from a 1,500lb block of glass at the 1937 Paris International Exhibition. His vases were deeply carved and etched, some with geometrical patterns alternating rough-hewn, polished and matt sections, some of which

86

86: DAUM NANCY Bowl in green with partly acid-etched design, c. 1930. D. 10, Mark DAUM NANCY. Broadfield House Glass Museum, Kingswinford; 87: DAUM NANCY Tinted vase with internal irregular bubbles applied with mauve glass bunches of grapes on stylised branches in black glass, the applied mauve foot with a black border, c. 1919-22. Executed by Eugène Galle from a model by Emile Wirtz. H. 15cm, Marks DAUM NANCY and Cross of Lorraine. Robert Zehil, Private Collection, Monaco

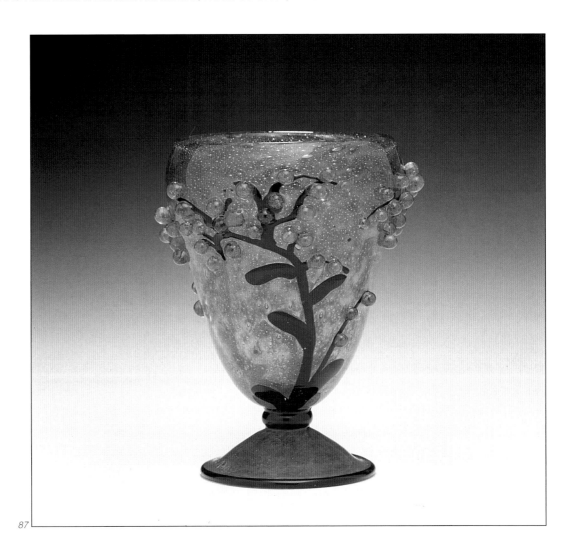

87

88

88: *VERRERIE SCHNEIDER Jug in mottled yellow glass cased in red and orange and acid-etched with a stylised floral design, c. 1930. H. 15, Mark Charder. Broadfield House Glass Museum, Kingswinford;* **89:** *VERRERIE SCHNEIDER Cased vase with orange and green mottling, stylised red poppies with applied black filaments and wheel-carved centres, c. 1920. H. 37.5, Mark Schneider. Robert Zehil, Private Collection, Monaco*

89

90

91

92

were stained or coloured. Each is unique. He received his second medal as Best Worker of France in 1927, and the *Légion d'Honneur* in 1931. During the German occupation in the Second World War he executed a number of official orders, the most notorious being a glass sword, two metres high, offered by the city of Nancy to Marshal Pétain, President of Vichy France. In 1944 Colotte was found guilty of collaboration with the enemy, was imprisoned, and had all his property confiscated. After his release he worked as a jeweller and executed a few portraits on glass, but died penniless.

JEAN LUCE (1895-1964) was not a glassworker, but a designer. He worked in his father's retail tableware shop until 1923, eventually opening his own shop. He designed porcelain and glassware, enamelled at first, then engraved and etched, its surface sometimes mirrored. Adopting very sober decorative motifs, he designed matched sets of glass and porcelain, the decoration subtly transformed from item to item. His designs for glass and porcelain for the *Normandie* liner so pleased the company that they were adopted for all their liners.

MARCEL GOUPY (1886-1954) was also primarily a designer, having studied architecture, sculpture and interior decoration at the National School of Decorative Arts in Paris, but he soon became an accomplished painter, silversmith and jeweller and began to enamel on glass. In 1919 Geo. Rouard took over the former *A La Paix* retail store run by Jules Mabut, and he hired Goupy to run the decorating shop. Rouard exhibited glass by Luce, Goupy, Marinot, Navarre, Thuret, Sala, Despret, Décorchement, Lalique, Baccarat, Gallé and Saint-Louis as well as ceramics by Decoeur, Mayodon, Delaherche and Lenoble. Goupy designed glass vases, decanters, lemonade and liqueur sets, some of which had small enamelled motifs while others had elaborate enamelled

designs, often enamelled inside as well as outside. He hired as his assistant Auguste Heiligenstein, who executed the enamelling as designed by Goupy. All these items were signed Goupy, who refused to allow Heiligenstein to exhibit his own works under his own name, leading to his departure after about two years. On the death of Rouard in 1929, his son appointed Goupy artistic director, a position he retained until his own death in 1954. Goupy went on designing and exhibited regularly. It is not known if he did any of his own enamelling, but he certainly had a team of decorators that included skilled enamellers. Much of his time was taken up with the administration of the showroom.

AUGUSTE HEILIGENSTEIN (1891-1976) was born in Paris, son of Alsations who had fled the German annexation in 1870. At the age of thirteen he was apprenticed to the Legras glassworks, leaving two years later to join the Prestat workshop as a porcelain decorator. Three years later he moved to Baccarat, left after four years when refused a rise, and joined an advertising firm where he learned to design and draw posters. Called up for military service in 1912, the outbreak of war two years later extended his military career until 1919. During this period he became a balloon observer and then an aeroplane pilot, receiving the military *Légion d'Honneur* for heroic conduct. A brief stint in a laboratory experimenting with new translucent enamels was followed in about 1920 by a job as Goupy's assistant, but he was expected to execute his boss's designs with no prospect of exhibiting works under his own name. Jean Mayodon, professor of Ceramics at the School of Applied Arts, whose works were on view in the Rouard showroom, introduced him to a former pupil, Odette Chatrousse, and she invited him to work in her studio. Heiligenstein had become friendly with Paul

93

Daum in the army, and he began to design shapes for Daum while Paul sent him various samples of glass to experiment with enamels. He was also artistic director of the Leune works, designing mass produced models of colourful enamels applied cold to hanging shapes, vases and bowls. In his own time he executed unique vessels which were enamelled all over in translucent enamels mixed with gilt, exhibiting widely and receiving several Gold Medals. In 1923 he married Odette Chatrousse, with whom he was frequently to work on individual ceramics. His clients by then included Lord Rothermere and the King of Siam; and he executed a dressing table set based on the Ballets Russe designs of Leon Bakst for Mrs Florence Blumenthal, an extremely wealthy American philanthropist.

JULES HABERT-DYS (1850-1928) was born in Fresnes to very poor, virtually illiterate parents. He spent years studying ceramics, drawing and painting. and provided the magazine L'Art with 500 drawings between 1882 and 1887, illustrated some books and decorated others, exhibited etchings, published albums of decorative designs, became artistic director of Lemercier, the art publishers and, in 1907, was appointed professor of drawing at the National School of Decorative Arts. With the occasional assistance of his son-in-law, a silversmith, he designed and made a series of intricately conceived and exquisitely executed silver boxes, vases, and other objects, often in combination with ivory, gold, horn, ebony, pearls, semi-precious stones and other metals. He then began to experiment with glass. His first bottles using a marquetry technique were exhibited in 1910 but he sold half the patent to the Lenthéric perfume firm and a change in its direction prevented him from using it again. He then went back to his experiments, and this time produced multi-layered

vases and other vessels using alternating transparent colourless and coloured glass, sometimes as many as six layers in different colours; the whole was then partly covered in torn shreds of rough metal, so that the colours of the glass would suddenly appear in the spaces between the metal craters. He exhibited these vases at the 1913 Salon and was awarded a Gold Medal. The outbreak of war in 1914 signalled the end of his practical work, and he spent the rest of his life designing things he never executed, failing health only permitting him to teach.

The Daum glassworks in the 1920s went through a particularly creative period under the artistic control of PAUL DAUM, third son of Auguste. He continued the production of some prewar designs but, under the influence of his friend Marinot, he also initiated a wide range of solid coloured vases - deeply acid-etched, sand-blasted or wheel-carved with abstract, geometric patterns or subtle linear intaglio-cut animals or plants - chunky table lamps and hanging lights. He produced reticulated vases and bowls in which coloured glass with metal foil inclusions was blown into wrought iron frames by Majorelle, Edgar Brandt or André Groult. Some transparent vases incorporating bubbling, streaking and metallic oxides had cabochons or complete trailings applied to the surface representing branches, bunches of fruit or trees or even abstract patterns.

During the German occupation of France in the Second World War the Daum works were closed down. Paul Daum was deported to a concentration camp, where he died in 1944. After the war the Daum family reopened the factory, concentrating on crystal with a high lead content, and later reintroduced pâte de verre. The brothers ERNEST (1877-1937) and CHARLES SCHNEIDER (1881-1953) moved to Nancy in 1881,

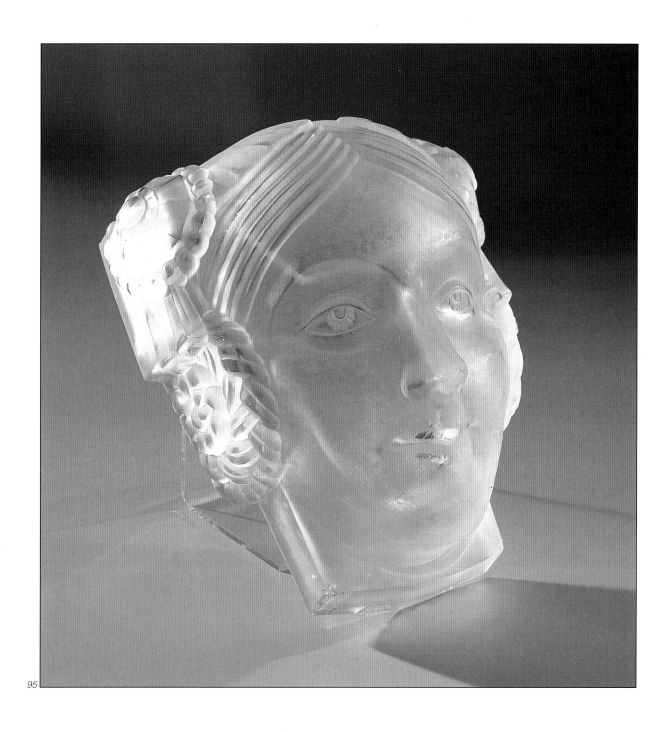

95

94: *SABINO Opalescent glass standing nude female figure* Reveil *(model no. 8549), c.1932. H.17.8. Victor Arwas Collection, London;* **95**: *SABINO Wall light cover in white frosted glass, c. 1930. H. 25.5, Marks* SABINO 4684 PARIS DEPOSE. *The Crafts Centre, Middlesbrough Borough Coucil*

96

97

Ernest joining the commercial section at Daum in 1902 while Charles became a freelance designer for the glassworks; he even designed at least one *pâte de verre* item executed by Walter. Ernest did not get on with Auguste Daum's sons, Jean, who became commercial director in 1909 on his father's death, and Paul. The compensation he received on leaving, his and his brother's savings and a loan from a friend enabled them to reopen an old glassworks at Epinay-sur-Seine, close to Paris. Taking on friends from the Daum and Muller, they no sooner started than they were all mobilised.

After the war the Verrerie Schneider poured out new designs, employing two chemists to devise new bright colours, including tango, a reddish-orange shade that swept through ceramics, plastics and dress fabrics. They were soon supplying all the French retail store design studios, exhibiting at all the Salons and showing permanently in their own showroom as well as those of Geo. Rouard, Delvaux and Damon. Using all the twenties' techniques, they produced colourful, internally decorated vessels, frequently with surface applications and intaglio-cutting. Charles, who designed most models, liked the idea of reconciling Art Nouveau and Art Deco sensibilities and techniques. One of his most successful concepts was to fashion an Art Deco vase padded on the side with a section of contrasting coloured glass which was intricately wheel-carved as a naturalistic Art Nouveau flower. As these were expensive and time-consuming to execute, he devised a new range of *cameo* vases, acid-etched in floral, animal or insect patterns in a stylised, contemporary manner. This range, complete with its own separate showroom under the control of their sister, Ernestine Schneider, was called Le Verre Français, occasionally with the signature *Charder*, a contraction of CHARles schneiDER.

Dr. Gregor Paulsson, writing on *Design and Mass Production*, explained the Scandinavian approach: "In order to convince the manufacturers of the importance of artistic quality in their products, we had to consider the economic basis of production. We insisted that the competition by means of low price and low quality should be regarded as an infantile stage of industrialism. It is not enough to bring the artist and manufacturer together: both parties must accommodate themselves to new conditions. The manufacturer must depart from his usual custom; he must give the artist a place in the schedule of his production. It is not enough to buy patterns; they are of no use by themselves, rather they do harm. The artist must be in the factory, and not as a hand but as a staff officer. He must have responsibility and he must have freedom. He cannot make designs for three hundred and sixty-five days of the year, he must have leisure for inspiration. Most of our factories, therefore, require the artists to work only half the time.

In the second place, the manufacturer must have patience. The first year's work is never good; the designs on paper may be so, but not the products. It is only when the artist has become accustomed to the technique, the materials, and other conditions that the products are good.

In the third place, the right artist must be secured, and I shall now try to indicate the most important points of our policy in this respect. As a rule we do not employ the students of the arts and crafts schools as leading artists in factories. We have found that only in a few cases have they sufficient capacity. The place of the great mass of the students of arts and crafts schools is as assistant-designers to the artists, as factory foremen or as skilled artisans for special work. The creation of

98

new models is so important that only the very best men should be permitted to make them. So, instead of using the average designer to do this work, we try for the best artist that we can get: painters, sculptors and architects. It is not, of course, an easy task to find an artist of high genius who is willing to change his work. Most artists are people who have studios and starve. But they have freedom, and they believe they are geniuses, and to go into a factory seems a humiliation. One must look, therefore, to the young intelligent artists with a progressive spirit and unsophisticated minds."

Swedish glassworks came to prominence in the 1920s, as they pioneered Functionalist glass: vessels designed soberly, perfectly fitted for their exact function, eschewing all irrelevant decoration. But in addition to this they exploited a highly original vein of art glass. Kosta, founded in Smaland in 1742 was the source from which many other glassworks branched out, including ORREFORS, which was bought in 1913 by Consul Johan Ekman of Gothenburg who wanted to produce decorated glass. He put in Albert Ahlin as manager, and was joined in 1914 by Knut Bergqvist, a master blower. He produced a few acid-etched floral *cameo* vases, some of which were designed by A.E. Boman, who had created some magnificent *cameo* vases along with Ferdinand and Anna Boberg, Alf Wallander and Edvin Ollers at the Reijmyre Glasbruk. Conscious of the need to take on "young intelligent artists with a progressive spirit and unsophisticated minds," the firm entered into extensive correspondence with various artists and, in 1916, SIMON GATE (1883-1945) was hired and, a year later, EDWARD HALD (1883-1980). Neither had any experience of working with glass.

Gate, son of a wealthy farmer, had trained as an academic painter at the Stockholm Academy, while Hald had travelled widely, studied with Johann Rohde and Henri Matisse, and had designed ceramics for Rörstrand. Both were shown the intricacies of glass creation, and both soon designed table glass. Gate also designed some tall, slender coloured glass vases, but spent considerable time with Ahlin and Bergqvist devising a new technique, which was called *Graal* (the Holy Grail). Gate's first *Graal* vase was a simple shape acid-etched in *cameo*, refired at the kiln to soften the harshness caused by the acid, then cased in clear glass and polished to a smooth finish. Gate and Hald designed very many *Graal* vases in increasingly adventurous patterns. When an engraving workshop was set up under Gustaf Abels, Gate and Hald devised highly inventive designs which were engraved in intaglio using copper wheels of every usable diameter: the deeper the glass was hollowed, the more prominent it appeared on the smooth side. Nudes, Biblical subjects, classical and mythological images of great intricacy appeared, Gate's being more complex on chunky glass; Hald's more amusing, simplified figures on thinner glass. At the 1925 Paris Exhibition, Orrefors, Gate and Hald were each awarded a Grand Prix while Bergqvist, Abels and two others received Gold Medals. Marinot's comment on the Orrefors display was: "*Il n'y a que ça*" (This stands alone). Gate and Hald returned the compliment by designing some glass inspired by Marinot.

In 1928 VICKE LINDSTRAND (1904-1983) joined Orrefors, designing for all their techniques, with a particular predilection for engraving shark hunters. He left in 1941, spent nine years designing ceramics, then joined Kosta in 1950 as principal designer. In 1930 EDWIN OHRSTROM joined Orrefors, and was instrumental in developing a new technique. Called *Ariel*, it consisted of sandblasting patterns onto the inner layer

99: ORREFORS *Covered pedestal vase with engraved decoration, designed by Edward Hald, 1926. H.36.2 , Marks Orrefors. H. 314 1926 and indecipherable monogram. Broadfield House Glass Museum, Kingswinford;* *100*: ORREFORS *Amethyst tinted liqueur flask and stopper, engraved with an intricate rondeau of nude women dancing, one playing the violin. Designed by Simon Gate, 1927. H. 24.5, Marks Orrefors Gate 234 1927 JGT. This model was first made in 1918. Victor Arwas Collection, London;* *101*: ORREFORS *Vases with engraved mermaid designs by Vicke Lindstrand: left H. 11, Marks OF L1221AISR OF GU66; right H. 16, Marks ORREFORS L1220. Kevin and Ina Harris Collection*

102

102: ORREFORS Octagonal bowl with Javanese dancers design by Simon Gate, 1934. W. 20, Marks G1346 1934. Kevin and Ina Harris Collection;
103: ORREFORS Ariel vase with cased Gondolier design by Edvin Öhrström, 1940. H. 17, Marks ORREFORS ARIEL 757 EDVIN OHRSTROM. Kevin and Ina Harris Collection; 104: left ORREFORS Vase designed by Edward Hald, 1930; centre and right KOSTA, vases designed by Elis Bergh, early 1930s: left H.16, Marks ORREFORS 1930 H248; centre H.33.5, Marks EB monogram 158; right H. 16.5, Marks EB monogram 250. Kevin and Ina Harris Collection

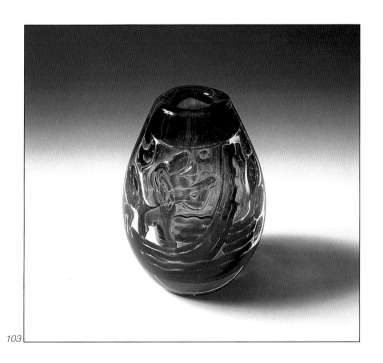

103

104

105

106

107

of the vase, then placing a transparent layer over this, enclosing the sandblasted air channels and forming patterns of air bubbles. Coloured glass could also be incorporated for variety. Several young designers have since joined the firm.

Curiously, the practice of employing an artist as outside designer briefly, but gloriously, occurred in Britain in the doom-laden years following the introduction of Lalique glass and the astonishing array of Continental art glass on display at the 1925 Paris Exhibition and later still after the 1929 crash. John Walsh Walsh, founded in 1851, was run from 1928 by the founder's great grandson, W.G. Riley, who invested money and time into researching a new range of thick-moulded glass panels which could be used in wall lights, ceiling fixtures, table lamps, illuminated panels or other architectural lighting. WALTER GILBERT, a sculptor who had executed the Great Gates to Buckingham Palace and the Victoria Memorial, the sculpture in the Great Reredos and other work in Liverpool Cathedral, and War Memorials in Ecclestone Park, Liverpool, Liverpool Exchange, Crewe, Troon, Burnley and other towns, was engaged to design the range, called *Vesta*. Using a multiplicity of shapes - square, triangular, five- and seven-sided - he designed a variety of animals and insects in relief. The most spectacular was a set of twelve panels, each 10 1/4 inches square, representing *The Twelve Labours of Hercules*. First introduced with great fanfare at the British Industries Fair, the Hercules panels were exhibited at the International Exhibition of Contemporary Glass and Rugs, organised by the American Federation of Arts, which opened in November 1929 at the Metropolitan Museum, New York, and travelled to Boston, Philadelphia, Chicago, St. Louis, Pittsburgh, Cincinnati and Baltimore, ending in Decem-

ber 1930. Curiously, they were catalogued 'Panels for elevator door' and listed as 'Executed by Walter Gilbert and W.G. Riley'. They were, presumably, not a commercial success as production was soon abandoned.

In order to encourage artists to go into industry and industry to employ them, the Board of Trade set up the Council for Art and Industry in 1934, which set up a National Register of suitable candidates, of which there were some 500 by the end of the decade. In the mid 1930s W. CLYNE FARQUHARSON joined John Walsh Walsh and designed a range of simple linear repeat patterns wheel-engraved in a contemporary, sophisticated manner. Launched in February, 1936, each vase and bowl was signed in diamond point on the base by the artist and dated. The patterns proved so attractive that the range was extended to include tumblers, decanters, jugs and other vessels. It was exhibited in the 1937 Paris International Exhibition, and at the 1939 British Industries Fair members of the Royal family purchased seven of his vases. These vessels continued to be made until 1942.

In 1933 Stuart & Sons, with LUDWIG KNY as chief designer, was asked to participate in an experiment to improve design by inviting a group of well-known artists to submit designs for breakfast and tea sets and for sets of glasses, the latter to be made by Stuart & Sons. They were to be shown in an exhibition at Harrod's in 1934, but as they were not all ready in time, a major exhibition was held a year later at the Royal Academy as 'British Art in Industry'. The artists were Gordon and Moira Forsyth, Laura Knight, Paul Nash, Dod and Ernest Procter, Eric Ravilious, and Graham Sutherland, and the exhibition also had work by Kny. Laura Knight submitted inventive, amusing designs for both glass and ceramics, as did Ernest Procter, while most of the other

109

108

designs were abstract, linear and graphic in their approach, Dod Procter supplying a witty, schematic water fountain. On the whole, the artists were more successful in their designs for glass than for ceramics. The results have great charm, though show some timidity of approach. The experiment was not a commercial success, and customers were blamed for their lack of adventurousness, but Stuart had not committed themselves wholly to it, having little faith in the project.

Thomas Webb & Sons hired Sven Fogelberg, formerly at the Kosta glassworks in Sweden, as general manager in 1932. His wife, ANNA FOGELBERG, and HOMERY FOLKES, a local architect, both produced interesting new designs, Mrs Fogelberg's primarily for sale through the Rembrandt Guild of Birmingham. But the longest-lasting and most prolific relationship between glassworks and outside designer was that between Stevens & Williams of Brierley Hill and KEITH MURRAY (1892-1981). Murray was an architect, born in New Zealand but trained at the Architectural Association in London. In the early 1930s, when architectural commissions were thin on the ground he began a relationship with Stevens and Williams that was to last until the start of the Second World War. As his agreement was that he would design glass exclusively for them, he spent two months of every year at Brierley Hill, working closely with the glassworkers, designing some 150 items for them a year; these ranged from simple coloured glass vessels, both modern and occasionally more traditional in shape, sometimes with a foot or handle in a contrasting colour, glass engraved with stylised figurative or abstract designs, enamelled vases, acid-etched vessels and others based on shape alone, which were clearly modern. The rest of his time was shared between designing pots for Josiah Wedgwood & Sons Ltd. -

whose new factory at Barlaston he designed with his partner C.S. White - and architectural work. Every piece of glass or ceramic he designed was identified on the base with a facsimile of his signature. He also designed a range of silver for Mappin & Webb in 1934, shown at the Royal Academy in 1935.

A totally committed import was that of the Ysart family. SALVADOR YSART (1877-1955) was a Catalan glassmaker from Barcelona who had emigrated with his family to Marseilles in 1909. When the First World War broke out he had just begun working for the Schneider brothers; when they were called up Ysart moved to Scotland. In 1922 he joined the firm of John Moncrieff in Perth. Encouraged by Mrs. Moncrieff, who also designed several vases, he began the production of a range of plainly-shaped vessels, mostly free-blown, internally decorated with swirls of colour, random or regular, often mixed with aventurine, gold flecks, mica or silver foil, the outer surface polished smooth. Most were vases and bowls, although some lamps were also made. As they grew up Ysart's four sons in turn joined the firm. Their range was called *Monart*, the first three letters of Moncrieff and the last three of Ysart. A very similar type of glass was made by *Gray-Stan*, a small glassworks set up in Battersea in 1922 by an Irish dealer in antique glass, Mrs. Elizabeth Graydon-Stannus. She ensured that all her pieces were made by hand, and produced an eclectic range of vessels, variants on nineteenth-century designs as well as decorated coloured glass, some with threads pulled in festoons, as well as others similar to *Monart*. Both *Monart* and *Gray-Stan* exhibited at the American Federation of Arts Exhibition which toured U.S. museums in 1929 and 1930. Both firms sold much of their production in America. Gray-Stan closed down in 1936.

110: *RENE LALIQUE* Vase quatre roses très en relief, *cire perdue, 1926. H. 16, Mark,* R. LALIQUE. *Private Collection, courtesy of Galerie Moderne, London*

111: *RENE LALIQUE Lidded vase* branches bourgeons en relief, *cire perdue, 1920. H.13, Mark on lid* R. LALIQUE. *Private Collection, courtesy of Galerie Moderne, London*

112: *RENE LALIQUE* Coffret anémones, *box with five glass panels of anemones, foil-backed on white gold, on silvered bronze carcass, previously unrecorded model, created c. 1910. W. 23, Marks* R. LALIQUE. *Private collection, courtesy of Colonel and Madame G. Ury (Galerie Moderne, London);* *113*: *RENE LALIQUE* Coffret figurines, *box with five glass plaques with design of recumbent female nudes, foil-backed with white gold set in a framework of burr maple. Model created in 1914. W. 31, Marks* R. Lalique. *Collection Mr. and Mrs. Vincent, courtesy of Galerie Moderne, London*

114: *RENE LALIQUE* Coffret monnaie du pape, *box with five glass plaques with honesty design, foil-backed with white gold set in a framework of banded mahogany. Model created in 1914. W. 31, Marks* R. Lalique. *Collection Mr. and Mrs. Vincent, courtesy of Galerie Moderne, London;*
115: *RENE LALIQUE* Coffret papillons, *box with five glass plaques with butterflies design, foil-backed with white gold set in a framework of burr maple, model created in 1914. W. 31, Marks* R. Lalique. *Collection Mr. and Mrs. Vincent, courtesy of Galerie Moderne, London*

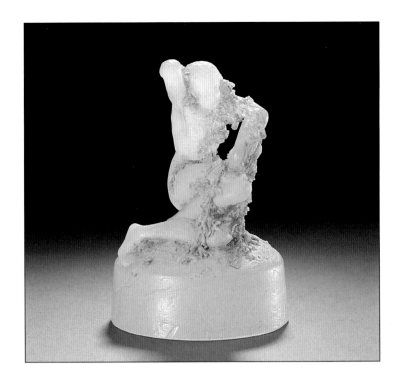

116: *RENE LALIQUE* Figurine femme assise aux feuillages, *cire perdue, in clear glass with brown patination,1921. H. 12.5, Marks* R. LALIQUE. *Private Collection, photo courtesy of Christie's, New York*

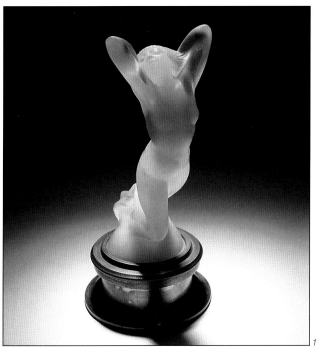

117

117: *RENE LALIQUE Car mascot* Vitesse *in opalescent glass. Model created in 1929. H.18.5, Marks R. Lalique. Collection Mr. and Mrs. Vincent, courtesy of Galerie Moderne, London;* **118**: *RENE LALIQUE* Grande nue, longs cheveux, socle bois, *Model No. 836. H. 41.5, Marks R. Lalique. Victor Arwas Collection, London*

118

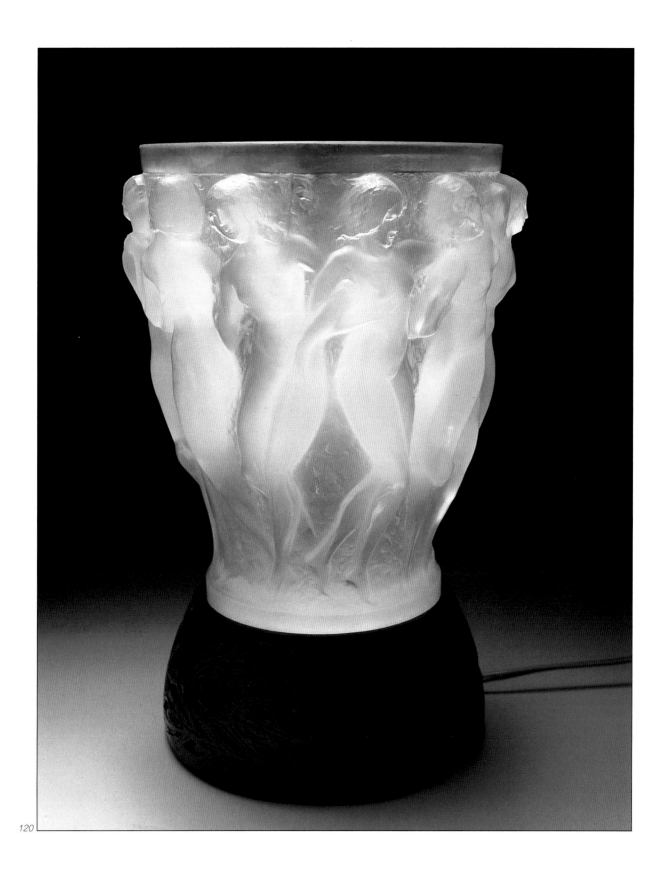

120

119: *RENE LALIQUE* Suzanne *in opalescent glass, model created in 1925. H. 23, Marks* R. Lalique. *Collection Mr. and Mrs. Vincent, courtesy of Galerie Moderne, London. This model also exists with a decorated bronze base equipped with light fittings;* **120**: *RENE LALIQUE* Vase bacchantes *in opalescent glass, model created in 1927. H. 25, Marks* R. Lalique France. *Collection Mr. and Mrs. Vincent, courtesy of Galerie Moderne, London*

121

122

121: RENE LALIQUE *Vase* grande boule lierre, *clear with moss green and brown enamelled patination. Model created in 1919. H. 35, Marks* R. Lalique, *Private Collection, courtesy of Galerie Moderne, London;* **122***: RENE LALIQUE Vase* tourbillons, *in clear glass with black enamelled highlighting. Model created in 1926. H. 20, Marks* R. Lalique. *Private Collection, courtesy of Galerie Moderne, London;* **123***: RENE LALIQUE* Surtout de table, *variant of the* Caravelle *model (created in 1930) made in 1938 with an additional design of seagulls to accompany the* Mouettes *service created in that year for the Royal presentation service. Intaglio moulded and acid etched in clear glass on a stainless steel stand equipped with light fittings. H. 47, W. 71 (including base) Marks* R. LALIQUE. *The inscription on the stand reads:* LA VILLE DE PARIS A LEURS MAJESTES BRITANNIQUES LE ROI GEORGE VI ET LA REINE ELIZABETH 29 JUIN 1938. *Courtesy of Her Majesty Queen Elizabeth, the Queen Mother.*
In July 1938 this magnificent service by René Lalique was presented to King George VI and Queen Elizabeth by the City of Paris at a reception at the Hôtel de Ville held in their honour to mark their official state visit to Paris. It consists of twelve place settings, four candleholders intaglio-moulded with a seagull design, and a massive illuminated centrepiece, Caravelle, *inscribed with a commemorative dedication.*

123

124: RENE LALIQUE Vase Oranges, clear glass with enamel patination in brownish black. Model created in 1926. H. 29, Marks R. Lalique, Private Collection, courtesy of Galerie Moderne, London; 125: RENE LALIQUE Perfume bottle méplat deux figurines, in clear glass, model created in 1912. H. 12, Marks R. Lalique. Private Collection, courtesy of Galerie Moderne, London; 126: CRISTAL LALIQUE Model of a horse's head in massive crystal, designed by Marc Lalique in 1953. H. 39.4, Mark LALIQUE. The Royal Collection © 1995 Her Majesty Queen Elizabeth

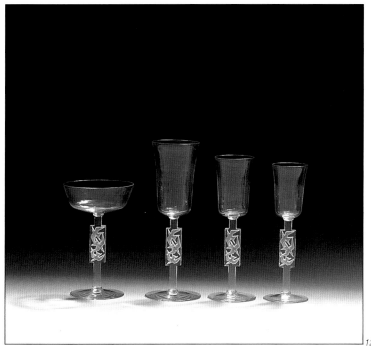
128

*127: RENE LALIQUE Candleholder on stainless steel base, part of the Royal presentation service, 1938. H. (including base) 17.8, Marks R. LALIQUE, Courtesy of Her Majesty Queen Elizabeth, the Queen Mother; **128**: RENE LALIQUE Champagne, water and wine glasses, part of the Royal presentation service, 1938. H. from left 15.9, 22.2, 20.2, 19.3, all marked R. LALIQUE. Courtesy of Her Majesty Queen Elizabeth, the Queen Mother; **129**: RENE LALIQUE Plate with etched coats of arms for the City of Paris and the House of Windsor, part of the Royal presentation service, 1938. D. 21.3, Marks R. LALIQUE. Courtesy of Her Majesty Queen Elizabeth, the Queen Mother*

129

130

131

130: *STEVENS AND WILLIAMS Vases designed by Keith Murray, c. 1935: left H. 38, Marks* Brierley *twice; right H. 20, Marks* Keith Murray S & W Brierley. *Broadfield House Glass Museum, Kingswinford, Michael and Peggy Parkington Collection;* **131**: *JOHN WALSH WALSH LTD.* Barry *vase designed by W. Clyne Farquharson, 1939. H.24, signed* Clyne Farquharson NRD 39. *Broadfield House Glass Museum, Kingswinford;* **132**: *JOHN WALSH WALSH LTD.* Pompeian *vase and separate internal flower holder, c. 1930. H.16. Broadfield House Glass Museum, Kingswinford*

132

133

133: STUART AND SONS LTD. Bowl with engraved design by Laura Knight, c. 1934. D. 29, Marks Stuart ENGLAND and DESIGNED BY LAURA KNIGHT. This bowl was exhibited at the Harrods' exhibition of 1934 and the British Art in Industry exhibition at the Royal Academy in 1935. Broadfield House Glass Museum, Kingswinford, Michael and Peggy Parkington Collection; 134: BAGLEY & CO. Vase with koala bear design in amber, model by Alexander Hardie Williamson, c. 1935. H. 20. Broadfield House Glass Museum, Kingswinford; 135: JOHN WALSH WALSH, LTD. Wall light consisting of three frosted glass panels in an Art Deco style metal mount, designed by Walter Gilbert in the Vesta lighting range, c. 1930. H.58.4, Marks on left panel G sc. R. fec. Broadfield House Glass Museum, Kingswinford

134

135

136

137

136: JOHN MONCRIEFF LTD. Monart *glass, clockwise from left: Vase in pink bubbly glass with vertical striped decoration and black foot, 1930s. H. 19.5, label* Monart Glass, VI.QC.492; *Vase with cased pink interior and pulled-up green, mauve and black surface decoration, 1945. H. 25. This* Monart Special *vase was made in 1945 at the Moncrieff factory by Paul Ysart in his own time and for his own pleasure and retained in his personal collection until July 1985; Vase in coral red glass with white lustred* Cloisonné *surface decoration, 1924-25. H. 15, label* Monart Ware, IX.C.18; *Vase in orange and red dribbled glass, 1920s. H. 22.5. Bowl in red and green glass, 1930s. D. 33, label* Monart Glass, III.0.52, Ian Turner Collection; *137*: JOHN MONCRIEFF LTD. Monart *glass, clockwise from left: Bowl in orange and yellow glass with regular bubbles and vertically spiralling decoration, 1930s. D. 18, label* Monart Glass *(code indecipherable); Vase in orange and clear glass with three multi-coloured swirls and silver foil inclusions, 1930s. H.33. This* Monart Special *vase was not intended as a commercial piece and was in Paul Ysart's personal collection until September 1988;*

138

139

Vase with green, blue and white lustred Paisley Shawl *technique surface decoration, 1920s. H. 23. Formerly in the Cyril Manley Collection;* Berluze *vase in blue bubbly glass shading to green at rim with vertical striped decoration, 1920s. H. 52. This* Monart Special *was a specially commissioned piece made by Salvador Ysart and said to have been a gift from Mrs. Moncrieff to a friend; Vase in orange, green and clear bubbly glass with aventurine inclusions, 1930s. H. 14. Ian Turner Collection;* **138**: *BAGLEY & CO.* Crystaltynt *pressed glass, 1927-38. H. between 12 and 19. Barbara Woroncow and Adrian Norris Collection;* **139**: *English pressed glass, clockwise from left: SOWERBY'S ELLISON GLASS WORKS LTD. Frog bowl in amber, late 1930s. D. 25.8; GEORGE DAVIDSON'S AND CO. Ripple vase in green/purple cloud, c. 1939. H. 17.3, Marks G. BRIT. R833445 AUSTRALIA 19221;* Eva *vase, design attributed to George Francis, c. 1935. H. 22.7, Marks Barbara L. Pigold; JAMES A. JOBLING & CO. Oval jardinière in* Opalique, *c. 1934. W. 41, Marks Rd No 794908. Private Collections*

140 & **141**: *LEOPOLD AND RUDOLF BLASCHKA Glass models of marine invertebrates, c.1870. Hancock Museum, Newcastle-upon-Tyne*

APPENDICES

The Glass Sea-Anemone Models made by Leopold Blaschka[1]

Susan Newell

The Trumplet, the Opelet, the Diadem Pimplet, the Latticed Corklet... the common names of sea-anemones fall strangely upon the ear. The study of these curious creatures is a relatively simple affair today with the aid of underwater colour photography and film, sophisticated aquaria and sub-aqua equipment. However, it is easy to imagine the predicament of the 19th-century biologist who, far from the sea, without the benefit of modern technology, was destined to witness the demise of his carefully collected specimens. In view of this, the idea of having models of these delicate creatures makes perfect sense. A number of such models exists in the collections of the Hancock Museum[2] in Newcastle-upon-Tyne. Visitors, however, often find it hard to believe that they are in fact made of glass.

The models were created by an expert glass decorator, Leopold Blaschka (1822-1895), who specialised in sea-anemone and later, flower models, at his home just outside Dresden.[3] He began making them in about 1860, and from 1870 was ably assisted by his son Rudolf (1857-1936) who continued working alone after his father's death. The Blaschkas developed a thriving business supplying models to museums and teaching institutions worldwide and the Natural History Society of Northumberland, Durham and Newcastle-upon-Tyne was one of the earliest institutions in England to acquire a group of them. The Council Minutes for the Society[4] record that a Mr. Brady bought glass models from a Mr. Fric of Prague in 1865 and the Committee Report of April 1866 records their arrival in Newcastle:

"The additions to the museum by purchase have been very few and unimportant, and except a set of glass models of the Actiniae of German manufacture, affording a means of representing a class of animals hitherto unrepresented in our Museum, there is nothing to which the attention of the members need be directed."

This underlines why Blaschka was important, for until he began to produce his models there was no way of demonstrating the three-dimensional shape, and the colour, of these animals in the absence of the living creatures. The publication of *A History of the British Sea-Anemones and Corals* by Philip Henry Gosse in 1860, however, already represented an important advance in the study of sea-anemones. It provided a detailed discussion of the different types, their behaviour and their habitat. Significantly it also included high-quality coloured prints showing them grouped in underwater rock pool dioramas.

Blaschka's first known commission for sea-anemone models was from the Director of the Dresden Museum, Ludwig Reichenbach in 1860. After seeing a collection of Blaschka's orchid models, Reichenbach realised that glass would be an equally suitable medium for models of marine invertebrates. It is probable that he was inspired to commission Blaschka directly as a result of Gosse's publication, as accurate and detailed images were then available, from which modellers could work.[5] Reliance on Gosse's prints, however, as the basis for the creation of three-dimensional models created a few pitfalls for Blaschka. For example, one specimen, depicted by Gosse as viewed from above, was interpreted by Blaschka as a low, flat model because he assumed from the print its form was essentially two-dimensional. In another instance a magnified detail of a tentacle has been understood as a complete anemone.

Professional or 'serious' biologists were by no means the only enthusiastic collectors of these models. A catalogue published by Leopold in 1871 *Marine Aquarien* is sub-titled *Zierde für elegante Zimmer* (Ornaments for elegant Rooms), and their purpose as teaching aids for institutions and museums mentioned only secondly. The 1885 catalogue, simply entitled *Blaschka's Modelle* gives a fascinating insight into how their business, by this time well-established, was conducted. It lists over 600 models and has a Preface in German and English written by Leopold himself. Institutions in Japan, Russia, New Zealand and India as well as many in Europe are given as clients and Leopold's justified pride in his international success is clear. No doubt due to past mishaps on account of the water-soluble animal glues and colours, he also uses the Preface to point out that the models are not suitable for immersion in real-life aquaria. "The models do very well admit of being kept in dry places; they are, however, by no means intended for aquariums, that is to say, they are not destined, to be steeped into water." Potential customers are also firmly advised against asking for discounts, "I have put the prices at such a low figure that I am utterly incapacitated to allow any discount whatever."

A description of the Blaschkas' working methods has survived,[6] written by Professor Goodale of Harvard University who, as the university's agent, commissioned large numbers of flower models from 1886. The Blaschkas used traditional lampworking techniques, choosing glass of different chemical composition depending on the way it was to be manipulated to achieve the desired shape. The glass elements were carefully fashioned with traditional tools and the model then constructed using, when necessary, wire, glue and occasionally paper or card. The finished models were cold-painted with minute care to match colours and create appropriate textures. Finally they were often glued to plaster bases coloured to ressemble their original habitat. This combination of superb technical skills, manual dexterity and artistry in glass painting applied to the making of scientific models was unique to the Blaschkas at this time and remains so to this day.

he Hancock Museum's purchase was evidently considered a success as more sea-anemone models were acquired a few years later.[7] Today they continue to serve their original purpose, allowing us to appreciate the variety and complexity of this extraordinary form of marine life, just as they also continue to bear witness to the genius of Leopold Blaschka.

Notes

1 I am indebted to Chris Meechan, Research Assistant, Sub-Department of Invertebrate Zoology, Department of Zoology, National Museum and Gallery, Cardiff, for allowing me access to his research on the Blaschkas, providing copies of the Blaschka catalogues and for advice and assistance in writing this piece.

2 The models are part of the collections of the Natural History Society of Northumbria. Originally housed in the Literary and Philosophical Society building in Newgate Street, they were subsequently moved to the newly built Hancock Museum in 1884. The Museum is now administered by Tyne and Wear Museums on behalf of the University of Newcastle-upon-Tyne.

3 "A Glass Menagerie: The work of Leopold and Rudolph Blaschka" by Chris Meechan The Glass Cone, Spring Issue, 1995.

4 I am grateful to Les Jessop, Keeper of Biology of Tyne and Wear Museums, for researching the Society's Minute Books and for advice regarding the models.

5 The link between Blaschka and Gosse was first established by Dr. Henri Reiling, Honorary Curator of the University of Utrecht.

6 The Glass Flowers at Harvard by Richard Evans Schultes and William A. Davis with Hillel Burger, 1992.

7 Minutes of the Council of the Natural History Society of Northumberland, Durham, Newcastle-upon-Tyne, March 3rd, 1871.

A Brief Dictionary
of proper names used in the text

Appert Frères, Clichy, Paris. The brothers Adrien and Léon Appert operated one of the most successful glassworks in 19th-century France. Their skilled glassworkers were able to produce a wide range of technically-demanding art glass, as well as glass for use in industry. In addition to designing and producing their own art glass, they made all the early glass designed by François-Eugène Rousseau.
14, 15

Argy-Rousseau, Joseph-Gabriel (1885-1953). A designer who specialised in *pâte de verre*, he exhibited his first models in 1914 at the Salon des Artistes Français in Paris. In 1921 he formed a limited company, Les Pâtes-de-Verre d'Argy-Rousseau, and from then on made a wide range of *pâte-de-verre* items including vases, bowls, night-lights and jewellery. In 1928 the sculptor Marcel Bouraine designed a number of models for Argy-Rousseau, mainly statuettes and bas-reliefs of nudes. The company's work is marked *G. Argy-Rousseau*, with Bouraine for those models designed by this artist. Production stopped in 1931 but Argy-Rousseau continued to make a small number of works, exhibiting at the Salon until 1952.
72

Art Deco. A style named after the first major international exhibition of decorative arts to be held after the first World War - *L'Exposition Internationale des Arts Décoratifs et Industriels Moderne* - held in Paris in 1925.

Art Nouveau. A decorative style which originated in the 1880s, based largely on organic shapes.

Arts and Crafts Movement. An attempt to revive traditional craft skills and improve standards of decorative design in the late 19th century, inspired by the ideas of William Morris.

Bagley and Co., Knottingley, England. Originally a bottle works, Bagley's made pressed glass from 1912. Their *Crystaltynt* coloured glassware was developed in the early 1930s. It was made in a range of Art Deco designs commissioned from London designers.
134, 138

Bakalowits and Sons. A major retailer of glassware in Vienna, this firm was particularly noted for commissioning glass designs from avant-garde designers carried out by such Bohemian glassworks as Loetz, and Meyr's Neffe.
58, 61, 63

Bakalowits, Professor Rudolf. A native of Graz, Professor Bakalowits designed a number of glass vases for Bakalowits and Sons which are known to have been made by Loetz. He was a member of the Wiener Werkstätte.
61

Barbe, Jules. An expert French glass decorator who arrived in Stourbridge in 1879 to work for Thomas Webb and Sons. He specialised in enamelling and gilding and the quality of his work ranks him among the most skilled glass artists working in England in the late 19th century. In 1901 he left Webb's and set up as a freelance decorator.
11

Bergé, Henri (1870-1930). Chief decorator at Daum from 1900-1914. Principal of their school for apprentice decorators, Bergé created many of the designs used at Daum over the years. When a *pâte-de-verre* workshop was established under the direction of Almaric Walter, he designed most of the models executed there too.
33

Bergh, Elis (1881-1954). A designer who worked for Kosta from 1929-50.
104

Billinghurst, A. Noel. Chief designer and glassmaker at Gray-Stan Glass, c.1926-36. He is best known for the figurative designs which he also engraved himself.
106

Blaschka, Leopold (1822-95). Born in Northern Bohemia, into a family with a long tradition of glass-working, Leopold Blaschka specialised from c.1860 in making scientific specimens of rare flowers and sea anemones in glass. He was assisted by his son Rudolf (1857-1936) from c.1870. See Appendix.
140, 141

Brocard, Philippe-Joseph (d. 1896). Trained as a decorator and restorer of antiques, Brocard made a detailed study of Islamic mosque lamps which, after many years, enabled him to reproduce exactly this type of glass with elaborately enamelled decoration. Brocard made a number of mosque lamps himself as well as vases, bowls and ewers decorated with enamelled arabesques and stylised motifs. He originally inspired Emile Gallé, and was in turn inspired by him.
9, 13

Bouraine, Marcel. A popular sculptor who also designed elegant, figurative models and plaques for Argy-Rousseau which were made in *pâte de verre* in the late 1920s.
72

Colotte, Aristide-Michel (1885-1959). Trained at Baccarat, Colotte eventually joined Daum in 1925 where he worked as a glass decorator. In 1926 he set up alone in Nancy, specialising in glasscutting. He evolved a technique of creating sculptural forms working from heavy blocks of crystal supplied by Baccarat. He would etch and carve his designs using hydrofluoric acid, wheel-cutting and grinding tools. His first sculptured vessels were exhibited at the

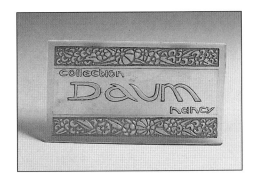

1927 *Salon des Artistes Décorateurs* in Paris and won him a medal as "Best Worker in France". In 1931 he received the *Légion d'Honneur*. In 1944 he was condemned for collaboration with the Nazis during the Occupation and moved to Paris where he later died penniless.
78

Couper and Sons, Glasgow, Scotland. Couper's developed a range of art glass called Clutha (after an ancient spelling of Clyde, the name of the river running through Glasgow) during the 1880s. The glass imitated antique Roman prototypes and is characterised by a bubbly appearance, frequent inclusion of aventurine or silver foil and fine streaks of opaque colour. Christopher Dresser and later George Walton were employed to design the models.
20, 21

Cros, Henri (1840-1907). Self-taught in the art of sculpture, wax-carving and modelling, from 1884 Cros began experimenting with the medium of powdered, coloured glass. His lengthy researches resulted in his rediscovery of the method of making pâte de verre. His subject matter was drawn from ancient Greek and Roman allegory and myth, and his work has a deliberately archaic appearance. He exhibited his first plaque in pâte de verre at the Salon of 1885.
71

Daum Frères, Auguste (1853-1909) **Antonin** (1864-1931). The Daum brothers took over and developed the glassworks owned by their father Jean Daum. Auguste worked as manager while Antonin, a trained engineer, concentrated initially on the production side. The art glass of Gallé, Léveillé and Rousseau, seen by the brothers for the first time at the Paris Exhibition of 1889, prompted them to change the direction of their own work, and from the early 1890s they began to develop and expand their art glass production. They employed a talented group of craftsmen, artists and designers, including Henri Bergé, Emile Wirtz, Almaric Walter and Eugène Gall. From 1893 they exhibited regularly at international exhibitions, winning numerous prizes. Daum glass demonstrates a wide range of decorative techniques including some new ones the firm developed itself.
29, 30, 33, 35, 39, 40, 41

Daum, Paul (1888-1944). Third son of Auguste Daum, Paul joined Daum in 1909 and slowly changed the style of its glass away from Art Nouveau. He pioneered greater simplicity in design, producing a range of transparent crystal and coloured glass vessels decorated with enamels. From the early 1920s a range of vases invented by designers such as Majorelle and Brandt was also made in layered glass blown into metal armatures. Influenced by the work of

Maurice Marinot, massive monochrome vases and bowls with acid-etched Art Deco motifs were produced from the late 1920s.
86, 87, 93

Davidson's (George Davidson and Company) Teams Valley Glassworks, Gateshead, England 1867-1987. Davidson's was one of the biggest glassmakers in England during the 1930s, making ranges of pressed glass in fashionable Art Deco style such as *cloud*, *ripple* and *jade* as well as many more traditional designs.
92, 139

Décorchement, François-Emile (1880-1971). Trained in fine and decorative art, Décorchement worked as a potter before focusing on *pâte de verre*. He began experimenting with the medium in 1902 and slowly developed more successful processes. By 1910 he had succeeded in making a completely translucent body which resembled gemstones. His new glass, now known as *pâte de cristal* was greatly admired at the *Salon des Artistes Français* when it was first shown in that year. Production ceased during the First World War but afterwards he continued to produce work which evolved from Art Nouveau-inspired motifs to simpler forms.
74

Despret, Georges (1862-1952). Despret began to experiment with *pâte de verre* in the 1880s, unaware that Henri Cros was working along similar lines. By 1890 he had begun to produce small items and he refined his techniques over the next ten years. His models are solid and heavy with a velvety matt surface and usually represent natural forms, especially the human face. He also employed a team of sculptors to produce models, including Georges Nicollet, Alexandre Charpentier, Yvonne Serruys and Pierre Le Faguays. Despret exhibited regularly in France and abroad from 1900.

69, 70

Dresser, Christopher (1834-1904). An artist, designer and academic, Dresser was one of the most important and influential figures in the development of British design in the late 19th century. He published works on botany, ornamentation and design. His views on form, function and ornament were profoundly influenced by a trip he made to Japan in 1877. He produced original designs for metalwork, furniture, pottery and glass which still appear modern today. His glass designs were made from c.1885-95 by James Couper & Sons under the tradename of *Clutha*. In these he drew on many varied sources for his inspiration, including ancient Rome, the Middle East and Peru.

20, 21

Farquharson, William "Clyne" (1906-72). Farquharson joined the firm of John Walsh Walsh Ltd. in 1924 aged eighteen as Chief Designer. He is best known for a series of elegant designs for cut glass vases produced during the late 1930s. The first, *Arches*, was retailed from the firm's London showrooms from 1936. His election to the National Registry of Industrial Art Designers in 1939 gives an indication of his status as a leading British designer. He continued to work for Walsh Walsh until they closed in 1951.

131

Feure, Georges de (1868-1943). A painter and decorative artist who established a workshop (*Atelier de Feure*) with the architect Théodore Cossmann in Paris. He designed furniture, fabrics, carpets, stained glass, book illustrations and posters. Only three models for glass are known by him, all date from c.1910.

85

Fogelberg, Anna. A Swedish artist who designed for Thomas Webb and Sons during the 1930s. Married to the manager of the firm her association with Webb's was curtailed by the break-up of their marriage and her return to Sweden.

107

Francis, George. London agent of George Davidson and Co., said to have designed their *Eva* vase.

139

Fritsche, William (1853-1924). Born into a Bohemian family with a long tradition of glass-engraving skills, Fritsche settled in England in 1868 and proved a highly talented and skilled glass engraver himself. He was employed by Thomas Webb & Sons and by the end of his life had acquired a legendary reputation. In addition to his work for Webb's he carried out freelance work for other Stourbridge firms and special commissions.

11

Gall, Eugène. A master glassblower who, from 1900, worked for the Daum brothers at the Verrerie de Nancy and remained there some forty years. The vases he executed are superb examples of the glassblower's art and technical expertise.

87

Gallé, Emile (1846-1904). Gallé was the most influential figure in the development of Art Nouveau glassmaking and the founder of the School of Nancy. His extensive education (he was knowledgeable in natural sciences, art history, Japanese art, poetry, as well as the physics and chemistry of glass) meant he was uniquely qualified to set new standards for glass design. Today his name is synonymous with Art Nouveau glass.

A love of nature informs all Gallé's work and he strove to reproduce as nearly as possible the beauty of natural forms in his glass designs. Impressed by the work of Brocard and Rousseau, Gallé's early work from c.1883 employs mainly enamelled and gilt decoration. However, he quickly progressed to designs using more complex cased, carved, cut and acid-etched techniques. A new range of his work shown at the Paris International Exhibition in 1889 was rapturously received; he was awarded a Grand Prix and Gold Medal and was made an officer of the *Légion d'Honneur*.

The glass blanks for his designs were executed to his minute instructions at Meisenthal at the Burgun, Schverer & Cie glassworks until 1894, when Gallé established a vast new glassworks at Nancy, the Cristallerie d'Emile Gallé. The craftsmen he employed there were supreme masters. It is thought that Gallé never personally executed his own designs, although he undertook research into new techniques and supervised the manufacture of his most elaborate models. Those are the best Gallé pieces. Much more industrial quality work was produced at the same time and continued to be produced until 1936 when the glassworks finally closed.

22, 23, 24, 26, 27, 28

Gate, Simon (1883-1945). An artist who joined the Orrefors glassworks as a designer in 1915. He invented *Graal* glass and designed many chunky shapes and different types of engraved and wheel-carved decoration.

100, 102, 97

Gilbert, Walter (1871-1946). A sculptor and metal worker who was commissioned by Walsh Walsh in the late 1920s to design the *Vesta* range of lighting glass in the Art Deco style.

135

Goupy, Marcel. Goupy worked in Paris as the manager of the shop owned by Geo. Rouard. His glass designs, which were sold in the shop, were usually of simple form with enamelled stylised figurative or floral motifs. For the most part they were executed by his assistant Auguste Heiligenstein. Goupy usually signed his work *M. Goupy* in enamels or gilding on the base or side. He continued to work for Rouard until his death in 1954.

81

Graydon-Stannus, Mrs. Elizabeth. Mrs. Graydon-Stannus, a dealer in antique Irish glass who set up a glass studio, Gray-Stan Glass in Battersea, London, in 1926.

Gray-Stan Glass, Battersea, London. The glassmaking studio set up by Mrs. Graydon-Stannus in 1926, and the name by which its glass is known. Gray-Stan is often brightly-coloured and similar at first sight to Monart glass. The studio also made reproductions of antique Irish and Venetian glass. Production ceased in 1936.

106, 108, 109

Habert-Dys, Jules (1850-1922). Originally a porcelain decorator, Habert-Dys studied at the Ecole des Beaux-Arts in Paris and by the early 1880s was an established graphic artist. He became Professor of Drawing at the Ecole Nationale des Arts Décoratifs in 1907 and began to experiment with glassmaking in his spare time. Habert-Dys produced multi-layered vessels, using alternating transparent colourless and transparent coloured layers of glass. They were awarded a Gold Medal when first exhibited at the 1913 Salon. The outbreak of the First World War marked the end of his practical career, although he continued designing until his death.

5

Hald, Edward (1883-1980). An artist who studied widely in Europe before arriving to work as a designer at the Orrefors glassworks in 1917. Hald created designs for elegant shapes engraved with whimsical subjects and others using the *Graal* technique. He became Manager at the works in 1933 but continued designing. His most creative period is generally considered to be 1917-45, although he went on working until his death.

96, 99

Heiligenstein, Auguste-Claude (1891-1976). Trained at various glass factories from the age of eleven, Heiligenstein worked as a glass decorator under Marcel Goupy for the Maison Rouard before going freelance in 1923. His glass is characterised by a complete covering of enamelled decoration usually inspired by Greek mythology or floral, geometric, stylised wave or cloud designs. He later worked again for various glassworks but continued to execute his own designs, usually on Daum blanks.

79

Hoffman, Josef (1870-1956). An Austrian architect and designer who became a founder member of the Vienna Secession group (1899) and the Wiener Werkstätte (1903). He developed a new functional approach to design, influenced by the work of Charles Rennie Mackintosh. His designs for glass, initially in the Art Nouveau style, are typified by elegant, symmetrical and crisp lines, prefiguring the Art Deco aesthetic. They were made by the Loetz and Lobmeyr glassworks.

59

Jean, Auguste. Principally a potter, Jean produced a considerable body of work in glass. He first exhibited a large group of glass vases at the Paris International Exhibition in 1878. His work is usually of Japanese or Persian inspira-

tion, although a rare group of freely-formed sculptural vases by him are also known.

10

Jobling's (James A. Jobling and Co. Ltd.), Sunderland, England. This firm specialised in mass-production of domestic glassware, lighting and heat-resistant glass (Pyrex) under licence. Inspired by the international success of Lalique, the firm introduced a range of art glass during the 1930s. They bought designs from French artists and had them made into three-dimensional models in Paris by Etienne Franckhauser who did similar work for Sabino and Lalique. Made in coloured, clear, frosted and opalescent glass (called *opalique* by the firm), Jobling's art glass was in production from c.1933-40.

91, 139

Knight, Laura (1877-1970). Although best known for her oils and watercolours of the circus and theatre and for her work as a war artist, Knight also produced designs for ceramics, enamels and glass. She contributed designs for glass (one of which was realised by Stuart and Sons) to the exhibition to promote better design in industry held at Harrods in 1934.

133

Kosta, Sweden. Established in 1742, this glassworks made Art Nouveau glass in the manner of Emile Gallé from 1897 to c.1910. In the 1920s and 1930s the firm produced modern designs by artists such as Elis Bergh. The glassworks became more significant in design terms in the period following the Second World War. Kosta Boda, as the glassworks is now known, is one of the most important producers of modern table and decorative glass in Sweden today.

104

Lalique, René (1860-1945). A leading designer of jewellery and glass, Lalique specialised in Art Nouveau designs for jewellery in the 1890s but later specialised in glass. He established his own glasshouse at Combes-La-Ville in 1909 and another at Wingen-sur-Moder in 1918. During the 1920s and 1930s he personally created a huge range of designs for glass including tableware, trinkets, vases, light fittings of all kinds, car mascots and jewellery. Today many of these have come to represent the essence of the Art Deco style and were emulated, both at the time and since, by many glassworks throughout Europe. Few factories finished their work to the standard of Lalique however, who used polishing, enamel staining, and wheel-carving to enhance the high quality of his moulded designs.

3, 4, 110-124, 127-129

Lalique, Marc (1900-77). Son of René Lalique, Marc took over the factory in 1945 on his father's death. He created designs for the firm from c.1930 onwards.

126

Léveillé, Ernest-Baptiste. Léveillé is known to have owned a shop retailing glass and ceramics in Paris from 1869. He became a student of François-Eugène Rousseau and assisted him as a glass decorator. In 1885 he bought Rousseau's workshop and continued to produce work using Rousseau's style and techniques. Léveillé also made elegant designs himself in the Art Nouveau style.

8, 15

Liberty & Co. This famous London store stocked both British and continental art glass. Works by Léveillé, Loetz and Argy-Rousseau were sold by them. The only British glass they are known to have sold is Couper's *Clutha* glass and Powell's Whitefriars glass. Both these

firms also supplied glass for mounting in Liberty's Tudric pewterware.

Lindstrand, Vicke (1904-83). An artist and sculptor who worked as a designer for Orrefors from 1929-40. He specialised in designs for engraving and is particularly known for a series on the theme of divers, fishermen, mermaids and sharks.

97, 101

Loetz Glassworks (Glasfabrik Johann Loetz-Witwe), Austria. The grandson of Johann Loetz, Max Ritter von Spaun took over the glassworks in 1879, greatly expanding and developing its technical and artistic resources. The firm's new ranges of art glass made a great impact when exhibited at, among others, Munich (1888), Vienna (1888, 1898), Paris (1889, 1900) and Chicago (1893), winning many prizes. Today the firm is associated particularly with the production of iridescent glass and Spaun patented the different processes used for many of Loetz's shimmering metallic finishes. Loetz also made work to artists' designs, including members of the Wiener Werkstätte, for example Josef Hoffman, Otto Prutscher and Koloman Moser. In Vienna Loetz's main retailer was E. Bakalowits & Sohn. Most Loetz glass is unsigned.

43, 57, 58, 59, 60, 61, 62, 63, 66

Luce, Jean (1895-1964). A designer of glass and ceramics who ran his own shop in Paris retailing ceramics and art glass from 1931. His glass designs concentrated on simple forms in clear or single-colour glass decorated in bold patterns, often inspired by Cubist art. His earliest designs were enamelled on glass, but he soon developed a preference for engraving and etching, as these techniques allowed him to exploit different surface textures.

82

RENE LALIQUE Advertising plaque. W. 7.8 Victor Arwas Collection, London

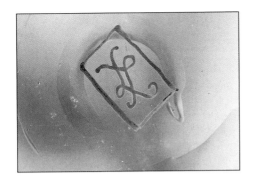

Majorelle, Louis (1859-1926). The main producer of Art Nouveau furniture in France. Based in Nancy, Majorelle frequently collaborated with Daum.

Maison Rouard. This shop at 34, avenue de l'Opéra in Paris was established by Geo. Rouard in 1919. It stocked work by many fashionable artists working in ceramics and glass during the 1920s and 1930s including Navarre, Goupy, Décorchement and Heiligenstein.

Marinot, Maurice (1882-1960). An artist who, after studying in Paris, returned home to Troyes, south-east of the capital, to paint. However, a visit to the glassworks at Bar-sur-Seine run by his friends, the brothers Eugène and Gabriel Viard, had a profound effect on him and from this time he channelled much of his creative energies into glass designing. From 1913 he learnt the difficult art of hot glass blowing in order to retain complete control of the creative process. His early designs were enamelled onto simple forms but he later rejected surface ornament in favour of internal decoration within the mass or deep sculptural surfaces, created through repeated immersion of the glass in hydrofluoric acid. Marinot's work was universally acclaimed at the 1925 Paris Exhibition of Decorative and Industrial Arts and from that time he exerted considerable influence on contemporary glass artists. He remains an important figure today in the development of the modern studio glass movement. The Viard glassworks closed in 1937 and Marinot returned to concentrate on painting and drawing for the remainder of his life.

77

Moncrieff's (John Moncrieff Limited), Perth, Scotland. Founded in 1865, this glassworks specialised in industrial glass. In 1924, however, it began to produce a range of art glass under the tradename Monart. This venture was the initiative of Mrs. Moncrieff and one of the firm's glassblowers, Salvador Ysart, who collaborated both on developing and creating the product range. Monart was made continuously until 1939 and production began again after the war and continued until 1961.

136, 137

Moncrieff, Mrs. Marianne Isobel (1874-1961). Isobel Moncrieff took an active part in promoting and designing Monart glass, made at John Moncrieff Ltd, the glassworks owned by her husband. She quickly recognised the commercial potential of a decorative piece made by one of the firm's glassblowers, Salvador Ysart, and with her backing *Monart*, as the new art glass was called, went into production in 1924.

Moser of Karlsbad (Ludwig Moser and Sons). Ludwig Moser (1833-1916) operated a successful glass decorating business in Karlsbad to which he added a glassworks at Meierhofen in 1893. The firm was incorporated in 1900 as Ludwig Moser & Sohne, with Ludwig and his sons Rudolf and Gustav as directors, and a staff of over four hundred craftsmen.

64, 65, 67, 68

Moser, Koloman (1868-1918). A Viennese painter and designer, he was a founder of the avant-garde artists' group, the Secession, and, with Josef Hoffman, of the Wiener Werkstätte. He designed jewellery, glass, textiles and furniture but is mainly known today for his painting and book illustrations.

58, 63

Muller Frères. The nine Muller brothers and one sister operated a successful glass decorating workshop in Lunéville from c.1895. Two of the brothers (Désiré and Eugène) had formerly worked for Emile Gallé's workshop in Nancy. The glass blanks were blown for them by the nearby Hinzelin glassworks at Croismare. They made a wide range of Art Nouveau glass, using many different decorative techniques, some which they invented themselves. Henri and Désiré Muller went to Belgium to work for the Val St. Lambert glassworks from 1906-7. The outbreak of war in 1914 forced the Lunéville glassworks to close, reopening again after the war.

34, 42, 44

Murray, Keith F.R.I.B.A., R.D.I. (1892-1981). An architect and designer who produced a range of vase designs for Stevens and Williams from 1932. Inspired by Swedish design, Murray developed new forms and allied these to contemporary motifs engraved on the surface of the items, thus utilising the traditional glass cutting skills of the factory workforce.

130

Navarre, Henri (1885-1971). Originally trained as an architect and sculptor, Navarre undertook several important commissions in bronze, stone and wood before turning his attention to glassmaking. Influenced by the work of Maurice Marinot, he produced heavy, thick-walled glass in simple shapes, often incorporating internal colour and granulations between the layers of the piece. His main outlet was the Maison Rouard. All his later glass was executed at the Verrerie de la Plaine Saint-Denis, near Paris.

80

Ohrström, Edvin (born 1906). A sculptor who worked for Orrefors two months per year from 1936-57. He invented striking, geometric forms in the late 1930s, some decorated on their internal surface by a turn-mould, a technique invented by him.

98, 103

Orrefors, Sandvik, Sweden. The Sandvik glassworks specialised in domestic glassware; however, art glass production, led by Simon Gate and Edward Hald was expanded and developed from c.1915. Their new work was greatly admired when first shown to a wide audience at the Paris Exhibition of 1925. Joined later by Lindstrand, Öhrström and Landberg, Gate and Hald made Orrefors the leading force in Scandinavian design during the inter-war period. Some designs created then are still in production today.

Powell's Whitefriars Glassworks (James Powell & Sons (Whitefriars) Limited), London. Powell's operated Whitefriars from 1834-1919 when it became a limited company. Under the direction of Harry Powell the glassworks made what is generally regarded as the finest handblown English art glass to original, aesthetic designs from 1880-1920. It finally closed down in 1980.

Powell, Harry (1835-1922). Harry Powell was the leading force at Powell's Whitefriars Glassworks from 1873 to 1919. He combined the roles of manager, chief chemist and glass designer and was responsible for directing the firm's attention to making art glass in the spirit of the Arts and Crafts Movement.

12, 18, 19

Rousseau, François-Eugène (1827-1890). Formerly an employee of the Sèvres Porcelain Factory, Rousseau began to experiment with glass from 1867. His early designs were realised by Appert Frères at Clichy, although he later produced his own glass. He was an inventive individual whose designs, often inspired by the new vogue for Japanese art, were extremely innovative and influential for the development of Art Nouveau glass. Ernest-Baptiste Léveillé joined Rousseau's workshop in 1877 as a pupil and assistant and he continued to work in his style after taking over the establishment in 1885.

7, 14

Sabino. This firm was established in about 1920 by Marius Ernest Sabino, a naturalised Frenchman of Italian origin. Based near Paris, it specialised in architectural light fittings and decorative items of all kinds in glass. Sabino created all the designs himself, which were then produced either by mould blowing or press moulding. A wide range of colour was used but Sabino is particularly known for his brilliant opalescent glass.

84, 94, 95

Schneider Glassworks, (Verrerie Schneider), Epinay-sur-Seine, France. The Schneider brothers, Ernest (1877-1937) and Charles (1881-1953), had both worked for Daum before they established their own glassworks in 1919. Charles had trained in Nancy and Paris as an

artist and he supervised the artistic and technical side of the business while his brother controlled the administrative and commercial side. Throughout the 1920s the firm sold art glass designed by Charles. His designs were simple and stylish, using a rich range of bubbled and mottled coloured glass, sometimes with cased, acid-etched patterns based on stylised natural forms as in their *Le Verre Français* range. The economic depression of the 1930s caused a severe downturn in demand, mainly on account of the U.S.A. ceasing to import art glass at this period.
88, 89

School of Nancy. A group of artists, designers and manufacturers who, in 1901, under the leadership of Emile Gallé formed a group devoted to the propagation of the French Art Nouveau style. Gallé was their first President while Augustin Daum, Louis Majorelle and Victor Prouvé were important members.

Serruys, Yvonne (born 1874). A sculptor of Belgian origin who worked in Paris and regularly exhibited her work there, receiving many public and private commissions. She was also one of a number of artists who provided models for Georges Despret's *pâte de verre*.
69

Sowerby's Ellison Glass Works Ltd., Gateshead, England. Sowerby's was said to be the largest pressed glass works in the world in the 1880s. The Works included an art glass studio from about 1870 to 1888. A small group of Italian glassblowers were employed there making a range of Venetian-inspired glass, as well as a more original group of items of uniquely individual design. In the early 1880s these products were exhibited by Christopher Dresser at his select shop, the Art

Furnishers Alliance, in Bond Street, London.
139

Sowerby, John George (1850-1914). Sowerby entered the family firm of Sowerby & Co. in 1871 as manager and colour mixer. His interest in the artists and designers of the Arts and Crafts Movement led him to introduce many new "aesthetic" models to the firm's range of pressed glass and to set up an art glass studio, an art pottery and a stained glass company within Sowerby's Ellison Glass Works.

Stevens and Williams, Brierley Hill Glassworks, Staffordshire, England. This large firm produced much Victorian-style art glass alongside more traditional cut glass items. In the late 19th century many continental glass artists were employed there. Later in the 1930s the firm revitalised its production of art glass with a range of stylish models created by the architect and designer Keith Murray.
16, 17, 130

Stuart and Sons Ltd., Stourbridge, England. This firm specialised in traditional cut glass production under the direction of the Bohemian glass artist Ludwig Kny. In 1933 Stuart's was asked to take part in a project designed to promote improved design in British industry. Artists were invited to contribute designs which would then be executed and included in an exhibition at Harrods. Laura Knight and Graham Sutherland were among the artists whose designs were made by Stuart's. Although the models did not go into production, they were much admired at the time.
105, 133

Sutherland, Graham (1903-80). This artist made designs for a wide range of

objects, including posters, fabric, china and glass. He contributed a glass design for an exhibition organised to promote better design in industry, held at Harrods in 1934, which was made by the Stourbridge firm of Stuart and Sons Ltd.
105

Tiffany, Louis Comfort (1848-1933). Son of the successful American retailer of luxury goods, Charles Lewis Tiffany, Louis trained as an artist and travelled extensively in Europe before returning to the U.S.A. to devote himself to designing art objects and interiors. In 1889 he had visited the Paris International Exhibition and was much impressed with the glass of Emile Gallé and his contemporaries. In 1892 he establish the Tiffany Glass & Decorating Company and financed the Stourbridge Glass Company, based at Corona, Long Island to develop his glassmaking interests. There, thanks to the formidable expertise of his chemists and glassblowers, a range of exquisite art glass objects designed by Tiffany, was produced from c.1895 under the tradename *Favrile*. Stained glass was also made and lamps incorporating stained glass were produced from c.1899. Tiffany exhibited his new products to overwhelming acclaim at the Universal Exhibition in Paris in 1900. From that year until 1916, when the U.S.A. entered the First World War, Tiffany & Co. was extremely successful. In the post-war period, however, his glass lost its former popularity as fashions changed, and the Corona glassworks closed down in 1928.
2, 46, 47, 48, 50, 51, 52, 53, 55, 56

Val St. Lambert Glassworks, (Société Anonyme des Cristalleries du Val Saint-Lambert), Belgium. This vast group of glassworks made glass of every descrip-

tion. As the new Art Nouveau style became increasingly popular in Belgium during the 1890s, a demand was created for Art Nouveau glass. The company then began to commission designs from well-known artists and in 1906 Henri and Désiré Muller were brought to Belgium to work for them, staying only for about a year. All the vases designed by the brothers have the mark *VSL* in cursive script on the side of the vessel within the design.

45

Velde, Henry van de (1863-1957). An influential Belgian architect, artist and designer who, in the 1890s, supplied glass designs in the Art Nouveau style to the Val St. Lambert and Loetz factories.

43

Walter, Almaric Victor (1870-1959). Walter was invited to Daum to establish a *pâte-de-verre* workshop there in c.1905. After a period of experimentation he began producing models to designs by Daum's chief decorator, Henri Bergé and by other artists. These took the form of a wide range of vases, trays, plaques and ornaments often decorated with animals, insects, plants and female nudes. The moulds for the *pâte de verre* were created by the lost wax method in order to remain as true as possible to the original. Walter did not return to Daum when the factory re-opened after the First World War, but instead set up on his own in Nancy, although he was allowed to continue making the models developed there. His association with Bergé continued up until the artist died in 1936.

73

Walsh Walsh (John Walsh Walsh Ltd.), Birmingham, England. This firm, based at the Soho & Vesta Glass Works, was run by the founder's great grandson Mr. W.G. Riley from 1928. He was responsi-

ble for the adventurous product ranges the company developed during the 1930s including Pompeian, lustred glass, Vesta lighting ware designed by Walter Gilbert, and cut glass designed by W. Clyne Farquharson.

131, 132, 135

Walton, George (1867-1933). An architect and designer who during the 1890s designed glassware produced by the Glasgow firm of James Couper and Sons in their *Clutha* range. His designs are noted for their symmetry and elegant simplicity.

21

Webb and Sons (Thomas Webb and Sons), Stourbridge, England. In 1932 Sven Fogelberg was persuaded to leave Kosta Glassworks to manage the Dennis Glass Works of Thomas Webb and Sons. He radically improved productivity and broadened the firm's range of products, importing continental working methods and staff. European and British designers were also employed to produce artistic glass to supplement the ranges of traditional cut glass which were the mainstay of the firm's production.

11, 107

Wiener Werkstätte. A craft studio founded in Vienna in 1903 by Josef Hoffman and Koloman Moser who were members of the avant-garde group of Viennese artists known as the Secession. It specialised in the design and production of metalwork, jewellery, furniture, textiles and leatherwork.

Williamson, Alexander Hardie (1907-94). Principally a graphic artist specialising in children's books, Williamson also designed textiles and glass. For many years he supplied the Ravenshead Factory in St. Helen's with designs for industrially-made glass and in the 1930s

he is known to have also produced six designs in the Art Deco style for the Yorkshire firm of Bagley's.

134, 138

Whitefriars Glassworks, see **Powell & Sons Ltd**.

Ysart, Paul born 1904. Trained by his father, Salvador, Paul Ysart became an accomplished glassblower in his own right. He was the only one of the four brothers to remain at John Moncrieff Ltd. after the Second World War. All post-war Monart glass was made by him until the company changed hands in 1961 and production ceased.

136, 137

Ysart, Salvador (1878-1955). An experienced glassblower of Spanish origin, Ysart had worked at various glassworks in France, including the Verrerie Schneider, before arriving with his four sons to work at John Moncrieff Ltd. in Perth. His skill in handling colour and manipulating form (no doubt acquired during his period in France) was put to good use in his development of the firm's range of art glass, Monart, with the active support of Mrs. Isobel Moncrieff, the owner's wife. From 1924, a wide range of decorative techniques was used including opaque enamel colours, lustring, aventurine inclusions, and manipulated bubble effects. However, the more elaborate techniques developed by Ysart were made increasingly less from c.1930 due to their expense, and more highly coloured, crystal-cased work was produced.

136, 137

Glossary

Acid-etching A simplified process for making cameo glass. A vessel of two or more layers of cased glass has a design drawn on it, then part covered with a protective varnish. It is then immersed in hydrofluoric acid, which attacks the exposed parts and forms the pattern.

Annealing The process whereby glass vessels are allowed to cool slowly and uniformly in a special reducing kiln called a lehr, thus avoiding the build up of stresses in the glass by too rapid cooling.

Ariel A technique developed at the Orrefors glassworks in Sweden by Edvin Öhrström and Vicke Lindstrand with the master glass-blower Gustav Bergkvist. It is based on the *Graal* technique developed at the works in 1916. This involved blowing a clear bubble of glass which was then cased and a design created by the use of acid-etching, sand-blasting or direct cutting. The vessel is then slowly reheated, its edges softening in the process, and the exterior then re-cased in clear glass. The *Ariel* technique also incorporates trapped air into the design of a layer or layers of coloured glass.

Aventurine Metallic particles suspended within the glass body, simulating aventurine quartz.

Berluze A type of vase with an elongated stem and small bulbous base frequently made by Daum and Muller Frères in the 1890s. An example was later made by Salvador Ysart in *Monart* glass.

Blow-moulded glass Vessels made by blowing molten glass into a mould.

Cabochon A convex blob of glass applied to the side of the vessel for decoration. Sometimes made of coloured glass or of clear glass placed over a metallic foil to give it colour.

Cameo glass Vessels of two or more cased layers of glass in which the outer layer (or layers) are carved or etched so as to leave a design in shallow relief .

Cased glass Vessels made of two or more layers of glass of different colour.

Cire perdue The French for "lost wax". This is a process in which a model is carved in wax then has a mould built up around it. When this is heated, the wax melts and runs out through small holes in the base of the mould, which is thus left with the exact contours of the original wax model. The mould can then be filled with molten glass or bronze which, on cooling, appears as an exact replica of its original model. Some moulds are reusable, others are destroyed when opened.

Clutha (an old name for the River Clyde which runs through Glasgow in Scotland) The name given to a range of art glass produced at the Glasgow glassworks of James Couper and Sons from c.1885-1905. It imitated ancient Roman or Venetian glass and ranged in colour from green, brown, amber to pink, usually with a bubbly appearance, often streaked with white, red, blue and aventurine. *Clutha* glass was sold by Liberty & Co.

Crackled Glass A decorative network of hairline cracks within the body of the glass, produced by rapid cooling.

Crystaltynt The name given to a range of coloured glassware introduced by Bagley's and Co. of Knottingley, England from 1934. A group of Art Deco inspired designs were available in matt satin and clear green, blue, amber or pink glass.

Cypriote Glass A type of *Favrile* glass made by Tiffany imitating the natural surface decay and corrosion found in ancient Greek, Roman and Egyptian glass that has been buried for centuries.

Encaustic painting A painting technique using colouring agents mixed with hot wax. Perfected in ancient Egypt and Greece, but subsequently lost.

Enamelling Coloured decoration sometimes applied to the surface of glass, made up of metallic oxides.

Favrile The Trade Mark registered by Louis Comfort Tiffany in 1894 for the iridescent glass, ceramics, lamps and leaded windows designed by him. *Favrile* glass falls into distinctive groups such as lava, reactive, paperweight glass, cypriote and cameo.

Fluogravure A technique devised by the Muller family consisting of enamelling a single or two layered vessel with rich colours, then acid-etching the vitrified enamelled surface into various scenes.

Gaffer The master glassblower who directs a team of glassmakers (or *chair* as it is also known) of different skills.

Gather The initial gob of molten glass taken up by the glass blower on his blowing iron.

Glory hole The mouth of the glass furnace where the glass vessel can be reheated during production.

Goose-neck Vases A type of glass with a bulbous base and tall, curving neck or stem. The shape is traditional, derived from Persian rose-water sprinklers.

Intaglio carving, etching, moulding or engraving the surface of glass. The hollowed out surface is contrasted with the polished surface of the vessel by treatment so that it appears matt.

Lampwork The fashioning of glassware from glass rods and tubes heated, softened and shaped with hand tools using an oil lamp, later a bunsen burner.

Lava A type of *Favrile* glass made by Tiffany with a rough, irregular, iridescent surface which resembles volcanic ash running with gold trails of molten lava.

Lost wax see **Cire perdue**

Lustre decorated glass Tiffany specialised in creating delicate lustred, surface patterns on glass (for example, his peacock feather vases). These were produced by applying blobs of coloured glass to the surface which were then combed into the desired pattern. When the glass was lustred, the applied decoration acquired a high iridescence, contrasting with the rest of the vessel. The lustring could be achieved in a variety of ways, including bathing the vessel in a wash of metallic oxides and exposing it to carbon monoxide fumes.

Martelé A type of shallow wheel-carving which imitates a hammered effect on the surface of metalwork.

Marquetry A technique devised by Emile Gallé and patented by him in 1898. Cut pieces of hot, coloured glass are inserted into the parison, then embedded in the surface by rolling on the marver. Once annealed the vessel can be further decorated by carving.

Marver A marble or iron surface on which the parison is rolled to smooth it.

Millefiore coloured glass canes are grouped together then sliced thinly and embedded in the surface of a glass vessel. The technique has traditionally been used in making paperweights, and variations were used by Tiffany and Steuben in art glass vessels.

Monart Art glass produced by the Ysart family of glassblowers at the Scottish firm of John Moncrieff Ltd. from 1924-61. (Monart derives from the first three letters of Moncrieff and the last three of Ysart).

Moss Agate A type of glass produced by Stevens and Williams from c.1888-1900, imitating hardstone. (It had been successfully produced in France by F.E. Rousseau and E. Léveillé since the early 1880s.) It has coloured streaks trapped between clear layers, the inner layer having a crackled appearance.

Opalique The name James A. Jobling & Co. gave to their opalescent art glass produced from c.1933-40 which deliberately evokes the name of the French glassmaker René Lalique, whose work they consciously set out to imitate.

Paisley Shawl The name given to Monart glass with crushed coloured enamels worked into swirls on the surface and then given a lustrous finish by exposure to fumes at the glory hole.

Paperweight Vases A type of *Favrile* glass made by Tiffany in which a thick layer of decorated glass was encased in a further smooth outer layer, trapping the decoration. Both layers were transparent coloured glass, the inside surface sometimes lustred, the outer sometimes carved.

Papillon (Butterfly) glass. A range of iridescent glass introduced by Loetz in 1899. It has surface decoration consisting of multiple, closely clustered, iridescent spots of raindrop shape, and was produced in many colours, for example, Candia-Papillon (gold), Ruby-Papillon (red) and Cobalt-Papillon (blue).

Parison The blob of molten glass taken from the kiln on a blow-pipe and blown into its initial, globular shape.

Pâte de cristal A form of *pâte de verre* that appears translucent and cristalline.

Pâte d'émail A form of *pâte de verre* which when fired has the appearance of unglazed porcelain

Pâte de verre Finely crushed glass mixed with a binding agent to make a malleable paste, and metallic oxides for colour, modelled like clay, then placed in a mould and heated just enough to vitrify the paste without having its constituent coloured sections run together. It may be heavy or light, opaque or translucent, matt or cristalline, depending on its components and time in the furnace.

Phenomenon A range of glass introduced by Loetz in 1899. It is characterised by iridescent glass threads pulled at random all over the surface of the vessel.

Pompeian A range of bubbly glass, distantly imitating old Italian glass as the name would suggest, produced by John Walsh Walsh during the 1920s.

Press-moulded glass Glass made by placing a blob of molten glass into a metal mould and then pressing it into shape by bringing down onto it a mould that describes the form of the inner surface of the vessel.

Reactive Glass A type of *Favrile* glass made by Tiffany which changed colour when reheated in the kiln.

Silveria The name given to a range of glass produced by Stevens and Williams for a short period from c.1900. It is characterised by a layer of silver foil trapped between two layers of clear glass with colour applied in the form of ground glass to the outer layer and surface trails of green glass.

Tazza An Italian word describing a vessel with a pedestal foot supporting a wide, shallow bowl.

Tears Tapering tear-shaped trails of glass applied vertically at intervals to the exterior of a vase or drinking glass.

Threading The application of fine threads of glass to the exterior of a vessel, the threads being fused to the surface yet often left in raised relief.

Tudric A trade name for a range of pewter items sold by Liberty & Co. from c.1900-10. Some of the designs were produced by designer Archibald Knox .

Straw opal Pale milky-yellow opalescent glass developed at Whitefriars glassworks by Harry Powell c.1877-79.

Verrerie Parlante (Speaking glassware) The name Emile Gallé gave to his glass inscribed with quotations taken from a wide range of poets and writers.

Vesta A range of lighting products first shown at the British Industries Fair of 1929 by the Birmingham firm of John Walsh Walsh Ltd. It was designed by the sculptor Walter Gilbert.

Wheel-carving The process of decorating the surface of glass by grinding on a lathe, or wheel, with a variety of metal discs of various sizes. The vessel is held up to the underside of the rotating wheel while an abrasive powder is fed onto the surface of the glass.

Select Bibliography

Arwas, Victor *Glass, Art Nouveau to Art Deco*, London, 1987

Arwas, Victor "British Glass" in the *Encyclopedia of Victoriana*, London, 1975

Baker, John and Kate Crowe *A Collectors Guide to Jobling 1930s Decorative Glass*, Tyne and Wear County Council Museums, 1985

Baldwin, Gary and Lee Carno *Moser Artistry in Glass 1857-1938*, USA, n.d.

Beard, Geoffrey W. *International Modern Glass*, London, 1976

Bloch-Dermant, Janine *G. Argy-Rousseau*, London, 1991

Bloch-Dermant, Janine *The Art of French Glass 1860-1914*, London, 1980

Capa, Giuseppe *L'Europe de l'Art Verrier*, Liège, 1991

Charpentier, Françoise-Thérèse *Emile Gallé Industriel et Poète 1846-1904*, Nancy, 1978

Cottle, Simon *Sowerby, Gateshead Glass*, Tyne and Wear Museums Service, 1986

Couldrey, Vivienne *The Art of Louis Comfort Tiffany*, London, 1989

Decelle, Philippe *Sabino*, Brussels, n.d.

Dodsworth, Roger "William Clyne Farquharson (1906-1972) A Short Biography," *Glass Association Journal* Vol. 3, 1990

Dodsworth, Roger, ed. *British Glass Between the Wars*, Dudley Leisure Services, 1987

Dolan Nick, *Davidson's Glass From Gateshead to the World*, Tyne and Wear Museums, 1993

Duncan, Alastair & Georges de Bartha *Glass by Gallé*, London, 1984

Duncan, Alastair, Martin Eidelberg, Neil Harris

Masterworks of Louis Comfort Tiffany, London, 1989

Durant, Stuart *Christopher Dresser*, London, 1993

Evans Wendy, Catherine Ross & Alex Werner *Whitefriars Glass: James Powell & Sons*, Museum of London, 1995

Gallé, Emile *Ecrits pour l'Art*, Paris 1908; Reproduction, Marseille, 1980

Garner, Philippe *Gallé*, London 1990

Gonzalez, Sylvie, ed. *Auguste Heiligenstein*, Paris, 1994

Hajdamach, Charles R. *British Glass 1800-1914*, London, 1991

Herlitz-Gezelius, Ann-Marie *Orrefors*, Stockholm, 1984

Hoog, Michel & Colette Giraudeau *Maurice Marinot*, Musée de l'Orangerie, Paris, 1989

Jackson, Lesley, ed. *Whitefriars Glass; The Art of James Powell & Sons*, Shepton Beauchamp, 1996

Janneau, Guillaume *Le Verre et l'Art de Marinot*, Paris, 1925

Janneau, Guillaume *Modern Glass*, London, 1931

Koch, Robert *Louis C. Tiffany, Rebel in Glass*, New York, 1964, 1966

Koch, Robert, *Louis C. Tiffany's Art Glass*, New York, 1977

Lalique, Marie-Claude *Lalique*, Geneva, 1988

Marcilhac, Félix *Lalique - Catalogue raisonné de l'oeuvre de verre*, Paris, 1989 and 1994

McDonald, Jesse *Lalique*, London, 1995

Moon, Karen *George Walton Designer and Architect*, London, 1993

Neuwirth, Waltraud *Loetz Austria 1905-1918 Glas*, Vienna, 1986

Opie, Jennifer Hawkins *Scandinavian Ceramics and Glass in*

the Twentieth Century, Victoria and Albert Museum, London, 1989

Pazaurek, Gustave *Moderne Gläser*, Leipzig, c.1901

Petrová, Sylvia and Jean-Luc Olivié *Bohemian Glass*, Paris, 1990

Pétry, Claude *DAUM dans les Musées de Nancy*, Musées des Beaux Arts de Nancy. n.d.

Polak, Ada "Edward Hald 1883-1980," *Journal of the Decorative Arts Society* 1890-1940, No. 5

Quesada, Mario, ed. *L'Arte del vetro*, Venice, 1992

Revi, Albert Christian, *American Art Nouveau Glass*, Nashville, 1968, 1972, 1981

Ricke, Helmut *Schneider Glas des Art Deco*, Hannover, 1981

Rudoe, Judy *Decorative Arts 1850-1950*, A Catalogue of the British Museum Collection,1994 (revised edition)

Rutherford Jessica and Stella Beddoe *Art Nouveau, Art Deco and The Thirties, The Ceramic, Glass and Metalwork Collections at Brighton Museum*, The Royal Pavilion, Art Gallery and Museums, Brighton, 1986

Schneider, Charles: Maître Verrier, Le Louvre des Antiquaires, Paris, 1984

Shrigley, Ruth, ed. *Inspired by Design, The Arts and Crafts Collection of the Manchester Metropolitan University*, Manchester City Art Galleries, 1994

Svenskt Glas 1915-1960, Nationalmuseum, Stockholm, 1987

Swedish Glass Factories Production Catalogues 1915-1960, Munich, 1987

Turner Ian, Alison J. Clarke and Frank Andrews *Ysart Glass* London, 1990

Wakefield, Hugh *19th Century British Glass*, London, 1961

Warmus, William *Emile Gallé, Dreams into Glass*, New York, 1984

Wettergren, Erik *Simon Gate, Edward Hald*, Stockholm, 1948